THEME GUIDE
Written by Gerard Kelly

With contributions from:
Pete Broadbent, Roy Crowne, Malcolm Egner, Debra Green, Mark Greene,
Neil Hudson, Rev Les Isaacs, Patrick Regan, Mark Roques,
Laurence Singlehurst, Viv Thomas, Paul Weston, Matt Wilson
and members of the 2012 Spring Harvest speaking team

CHURCH
△CTUALLY

How to use the Theme Guide

The Theme Guide is designed to resource your journey through the Spring Harvest 2012 theme, whether you are making that journey at the Event with our teaching team or afterwards in your own local context. The guide covers four big themes - each one a 'brilliant idea' implicit in God's design for the church. Each section - covering, at the event, one day of our programme - offers an exploration of one of these four 'brilliant ideas', giving background material and suggestions for discussion, further exploration and application.

At the heart of this Guide is a deep love for God's church. We want to celebrate together all that is good and beautiful and inspiring about this remarkable people-movement. And where we could do better, where the world could perhaps see more of God through us, we want to offer a gentle word of challenge.

We have asked a number of our friends around the UK church to share their perspectives with us, and in particular to tell us their story of where they have seen the church truly being 'God's brilliant idea'. We hope you will be encouraged as you read, just as we have been in brining these stories to you.

We pray that as you explore this important theme with us, you will know the presence and power of the God who has said that he will shine into his world, and that he will do it through his people.

Spring Harvest wishes to acknowledge and thank the following people for their help in the compilation and production of this theme guide:

Hannah Barraclough, Wendy Beech-Ward, Vicky Beeching,
Rebecca Bowater, Pete Broadbent, Graeme Bunn, Siân Clarke,
Jaqs Graham, Abby Guinness, Krish Kandiah, Ian MacDowell,
Alice O'Kane, Phil Loose, Kieran Metcalfe, Patrick Regan,
Ruth Valerio, Laura West & Paul Weston.

God's brilliant idea

"THEY LOVE JESUS BUT HATE THE CHURCH"

"DO I HAVE TO GO?'

"IF IT WASN'T FOR THE PEOPLE, OUR CHURCH WOULD BE JUST GREAT"

"EVERYTHING ABOUT THE WAY WE DO CHURCH NEEDS TO CHANGE"

"IF YOU THINK THE CHURCH IS BRILLIANT, YOU HAVEN'T BEEN TO MINE'

"I'M SO BORED"

How many times a day do Christians speak glibly, and uncharitably, about the Church? Without it there would be no faith to be part of, yet for many it is the very thing that makes faith hard to hold onto. And such is our recent experience of decline that we wrestle with the question of whether there will even be a Church in the nations of the West in the coming decades. Love her or hate her; believe in her or despair for her future - there can be little question that what happens to our churches in the coming 50 years will write a new chapter in the history of Christianity.

In *Church Actually* we want to bring two vital questions to the exploration of the Church.

» Firstly, what actually is the Church? How do scripture, theology and history ask us to view this God-shaped people movement, and how do those views affect how we see her future?

» Secondly, *where are we* actually, as churches, in the 21st century? In a culture that has largely lost interest in us but is increasingly vehement in challenging our long-held beliefs, what hope is there for our effectiveness in mission? Are we in unstoppable decline, as some have claimed, or is there new life yet for this ancient and historic idea?

Exploring these two questions involves touching on two distinct yet connected areas of study. The first is the theology of the Church, and is a field called ecclesiology. This explores ideas of just what it is that God intends his Church to be. The second is the study of mission, called 'missiology'. This is more a consideration of what God calls the Church to do: it asks what God's purpose is for the Church in history. In simple terms these two conversations can be expressed as two questions: what is the Church and what is it for?

Imagine you have been rummaging at a car boot sale and you discover a really interesting and well-preserved Victorian instrument. It is made of brass and polished wood, and seems to have some kind of spring-wound operating system. It looks like a camera but has no lens. It could be a phonograph but there's nowhere to put a record. You take it to an expert, who examines it closely, then says:

'You wind the spring here, then you feed a punch card into the mechanism here, and as a result it makes music here. It's a music box that plays songs "programmed" on the cards.'

The significance of this conversation is that the expert explains what the piece is by explaining *what it does*. The questions 'what is it?' and the question 'what is it for?' are intimately connected. Similarly if you ask an architect 'What is a window?' or 'What is a door?', the answer is likely to be in terms of what each *does* for the building. A window is cut into a wall to let the light in. A door allows people to enter and leave. The same is true in the ways the New Testament speaks of the Church. Sometimes the texts speak of what the Church *is* and sometimes they speak of what it *is for*. The *nature* of the Church and the *purpose* of the Church are deeply connected. It is in putting the two questions together that the full picture emerges. Ecclesiology asks of the Church *'what is it?'* and missiology asks *'what's it for?'*, and it is where ecclesiology and missiology meet that the fullest picture of the Church actually emerges. There is a vital connection between the Church and the mission of God, and rediscovering this connection may be the key to our survival and health as God's people.

Our exploration of the Church, then, will unashamedly ask both questions. In scripture and in our contemporary world we will consider what the Church is and what the Church is for, and seek out, in the connection of the two, a vision for our life together.

WHY THE CHURCH?

The very idea of Church assumes that there is a collective or corporate dimension to faith. It sees at the core of the faith journey a call for 'gathering' or 'assembly': for some expression of community. At heart this is a reflection of the relational nature of God himself. From the start, the biblical narrative asserts that God is not alone, and neither should humans be. We are relational creatures reflecting our relational creator. For many recent theologians, the call to form community arises directly and specifically from the nature of God as Trinity. Scholars such as the Orthodox Zizioulas, the Roman Catholic Ratzinger (Pope Benedict) and the Protestant Miroslav Volf are united in affirming the direct link between God as Trinity and the Church as community. Tim Keller suggests that:

... if from all eternity, without end and without beginning, ultimate reality is a community of persons knowing and loving one another, then ultimate reality is about love relationships ... You are made to enter into a divine dance with the Trinity.[1]

The forming of community is not an 'added extra' to faith but is fundamental to it.

Because the Christian God is not a lonely God, but rather a communion of three persons, faith leads human beings into the divine communion. One cannot, how ever, have a self-enclosed communion with the Triune God - a 'foursome,' as it were - for the Christian God is not a private deity. Communion with this God is at once also communion with those others who have entrusted themselves in faith to the same God. Hence one and the same act of faith places a person into a new relationship both with God and with all others who stand in communion with God. [2]

This allows us to make relationships central to our understanding of God, so that ecclesiology sits right at the very centre of theology.

'Community' is important as an integrative motif for theology not only because it fits with contemporary thinking, but more importantly because it is central to the message of the Bible. From the narratives of the primordial garden which opens the curtain on the biblical story, to the vision of white-robed multitudes inhabiting the new earth with which it concludes, the drama of the scriptures speaks of community. [3]

We are made to be together, to interact with others - and in the context of faith 'being together' is called the Church. Thus in Acts 1 and 2 when the Church is first formed, there is an immediate expression of gathered community. The Church is born in the form of gathering.

It is important to state from the very beginning that it is what this gathering *is*, not what it *does* that constitutes the Church. The very acts of being together; of acknowledging in worship who God is; of declaring his glory and enjoying his presence - these are sufficient to make us his people. But the purpose of this community flows quickly and seamlessly from its nature. As we gather, as we worship, as we come to know God, we find ourselves drawn into his purposes for the world. We begin to want what he wants. We are transformed to be more like him. Our ways of walking through his world are changed. Our actions flow as an expression of our nature. Mission is not a departure *from* worship but an outworking of it: what we do expresses who we are.

1] Timothy Keller, *King's Cross: The Story of the World in the Life of Jesus,* Penguin (USA), 2011
2] Miroslav Volf, *After Our Likeness: The Church As the Image of the Trinity,* Eerdmans, 1998
3] Stanley J Grenz, *Theology for the Community of God,* Broadman and Holman, 1994

MANY MODELS ONE MOVEMENT

Rather than settling on any one metaphor for the Church, the New Testament offers us a wide range of images. Scholars identify nearly 100 distinct images used to describe the Church.[4] Many of these are organic, drawn from the farming and fishing lives of Jesus' contemporaries: images of vines and fields; families and bodies. But there are also buildings and nations; cities bright with light or glistening in their jewelled splendour. Chad Brennan identifies the eleven most prominent New Testament metaphors for the Church as:

> » Branches on a vine, which is Christ (John 15)
> » God's field (1 Corinthians 3)
> » God's temple (1 Corinthians 3)
> » The body of Christ with all of us as the parts (1 Corinthians 12)
> » The bride of Christ (2 Corinthians 11)
> » The body of Christ with Christ as the head (Ephesians 4)
> » A family (1 Timothy 5)
> » God's house - with Jesus as the builder (Hebrews 3)
> » Living stones being built into a spiritual house (1 Peter 2)
> » A holy priesthood (1 Peter 2)
> » A holy nation, a people belonging to God (1 Peter 2)[5]

These different images have two factors in common. They are collective metaphors - they imply some sense of gathering or assembly - and they are rich in *purpose:* each points towards results, fruits or outcomes that cannot come into being without the coming together of God's people. This element of shared purpose - the goal around which the assembly forms and from which its sense of meaning is derived - is highly significant to the New Testament. 'The fellowship of Jesus' followers', Stanley Grenz writes, 'is not merely a loose coalition of individuals who acknowledge Jesus... Rather, it is a community of disciples who seek to walk together in accordance with the principles of the kingdom.' [6]

Church is a collective noun for *the followers of Christ who choose to journey together for the fulfillment of his purposes.* It is collective not only in the sense of the congregation but also of the Church's 'catholicity'. There is one Church, not multiple churches. To journey together in local, visible community is also to journey with God's people across the world. The Christian communities of Rome, Corinth, Jerusalem and Ephesus sought not only to express unity locally, as congregations of faith, but also to connect trans-locally, expressing the wider unity of the family of faith. Connection to the people of God across time and space is an important aspect of what it means to be the Church.

Whilst each of the different metaphors offered by the New Testament warrants study and exploration, we are going to take four - arguably the four most common images - and through them explore what being the Church means. In this we are not only looking for an original, New Testament sense of the Church, but also for lessons for the Church in our postmodern culture. We want to identify ideas and resources that can help us, today, to be the Church God intends us to be. The four metaphors we will explore, with the core meanings we will draw from them are:

(1) God's brilliant idea: Let them shine!
The Church as the People of God

(2) God's brilliant idea: Give them power!
The Church as the Community of the Spirit

(3) God's brilliant idea: Help them love!
The Church as the Body of Christ

(4) God's brilliant idea: Make them one!
The Church as the Bride of Christ

Each of these metaphors will give us a 'way-in' to what the Bible says the Church is called to be and how we can respond in our own time and culture. Our aim in exploring these metaphors is to celebrate not only what the Church is but what it *can be*. The Church is God's brilliant idea, and at its best it is the most remarkable, the most colourful, the most beautiful and the most redeeming of all human communities. It is a community of welcome and of healing; of forgiveness

4] Paul S Minear, *Images of the Church in the New Testament,* John Knox Press, 2004
5] Chad Brennan, *7 Principles of the New Culture,* http://thenewculture.org/articles/principles-2-cb/
6] Stanley J Grenz, *Theology for the Community of God,* Broadman and Holman, 1994

and of the second chance; a place of unexpected joy and unearned grace. At its best it is the family we all want and need. At its worst, it is the family we run from: the dysfunctional, controlling horror show that haunts our nights and ruins our days. But the answer to dysfunction does not lie in living alone. We will not be healed by running from relationship. Rather it is in building healthy churches, in creating communities of self-giving love, that we will find hope, for ourselves and for our world.

'The best argument for Christianity is Christians,' Sheldon Vanauken once wrote, 'their joy, their certainty, their completeness. But the strongest argument *against* Christianity is also Christians – when they are sombre and joyless, when they are self-righteous and smug in complacent consecration, when they are narrow and repressive, then Christianity dies a thousand deaths.'[7]

Can we become again the loving community God is looking for? Can mercy triumph over judgement in our lives and gatherings, so that the poor and the needy find the love they so long for? Will the meek receive their inheritance through us? We believe it is possible to answer *yes* to each of these questions, but that to do so commits us to a journey of prayer and work; to honest self-examination and authentic engagement with others; to seeking out the voice of the Spirit for our age. Jesus said that forces of hell could not prevent the building of the Church. He didn't say they wouldn't try.

But it is possible. It can be done. The Church, Lesslie Newbigin suggests, is called to be an 'explosion of joy' in its community.[8]

(handwritten note) THAT IT SHOULD BE SO; WE AGREE. THAT IT CAN BE SO; WE BELIEVE. THAT IT MIGHT BE SO; WE PRAY.

THROUGHOUT THE *THEME GUIDE* YOU WILL FIND THREE RECURRING BOXES:

Workout boxes are exercises and activities to help you explore the *Church Actually* material.

So What? boxes are applications, helping you to think through just how the *Church Actually* material might play out in *your* church and community.

Speakers' Corner boxes are comments from our 2012 Spring Harvest speaking team about the things they most love, and most struggle with, about the Church.

In addition we have included occasional **HOPEquotes** - comments and observations from UK churches engaging in shared projects under the 'HOPE' banner.

7] Sheldon Vanauken, cited in Leonard Sweet, *Carpe Manana*, Zondervan, 2001

8] "Mission begins with a kind of explosion of joy. The news that the rejected and crucified Jesus is alive is something that cannot possibly be suppressed. ...the mission of the Church in the pages of the New Testament is more like the fallout from a vast explosion, a radioactive fallout which is not lethal but life-giving" Lesslie Newbigin, *The Gospel in a Pluralist Society*, Eerdmans, 1996

contents

1
let
them
shine

let them shine
THE CHURCH AS THE PEOPLE OF GOD

In the simplest possible terms, the Church is people. 'Church' is the collective word for the singular term 'disciple'. As we journey towards Christ and onwards with Christ, we find ourselves in company with others who are making the same journey, and together we discover what following Christ will mean.

But the Church is not a random collection of people: it is people brought together for a purpose. God's plan for the Church is to 'shine' his wisdom through all those who follow Christ. God's intention is to *let people shine*, and the process by which he does this is called the Church.

You may not think of the members of your local church as people through whom the light of God shines. You may not see yourself that way. But the picture of the Church we are given in the New Testament suggests that this is God's plan.

The Church is the people of God, called to become like him and reflect his character and wisdom in the world. It is his way of getting things done. His way of showing love to the loveless, his way of bringing hope to a confused and frightened world. The Church is God's brilliant idea...

WHAT WILL WE DISCOVER IN THIS *CHURCH ACTUALLY* SESSION?

» That the Church sits right at the heart of God's plans for the world. It is the new human community through which he will shine his wisdom in all its constituent colours.

» That the Church of God and the mission of God are inseparably connected. The Church comes into being through God's mission, and God's mission flows out from the Church.

» That the Church is the Church *both* when it is gathered: for worship, disciple-making or other activities - and when it is scattered: dispersed into the million-and-one callings of all our daily lives.

» That the Church's job is not to spread the Church but to spread the kingdom - the wisdom of God applied to all the many issues of the everyday. The kingdom comes when God's will is done, and the Church is the means by which more and more humans become willing to do it.

» That 'equipping' is central to the life of the Church - each member of Christ's body being given what they need, to do what God has called them to do.

» That God's mission through the Church is 'prismatic' - the light of God breaking out in our lives into its many colours.

We will discover that the Church is God's 'Plan A', called to fulfill his purposes in the world. She is God's brilliant idea, and though she may fail and falter, God's plans will ultimately triumph through her.

CITIZENS' ASSEMBLY

The word 'ecclesiology' is derived from the Greek word most commonly used in the New Testament to describe the Church: *ekklesia*, meaning 'assembly'. In Acts 19:32; 39; 41 it is used to describe 'the citizens of a given community called together to tend to city affairs.'[9] Individuals with a shared identity (as citizens) come together to pursue a shared purpose (the concerns of their city). Similarly, the Church assembles those who self-identify as Christ's followers and come together to pursue the purposes Christ has bequeathed them. But *ekklesia* is more than this. It also provides a link back to the Old Testament and the nation of Israel.

The Jewish scholars who created the Septuagint - the Greek translation of the Hebrew scriptures - chose *ekklesia* to render the Hebrew word *qahal* ('assembly'). This is the word used in the Old Testament to refer to Israel as the 'congregation' or 'assembly of the Lord.'[10] *Ekklesia,* then, became the designation for 'the people of God' in the New Testament. In some senses this was seen as a continuation of the Old Testament idea of the 'people of God', and in other senses as a departure from it. The birth of the Church at Pentecost marks a new phase in the purposes of God: just as God was with the Hebrew slaves as they moved towards freedom and established the nation of Israel, so he will journey with his people now as the Church forms. In this way the early Christians 'linked themselves as the followers of Jesus to what God had begun in the wilderness with the nation of Israel.'[11]

The means of this identity was then, and is now, baptism. In baptism the individual is joined to 'the people of God'. The Church is not an ethnically or racially defined community, nor is it simply a collection of 'assemblies' all added together - it is the community of all baptised believers. To be part of the people of God you do not need to be born in a certain place or at a certain time, nor do you need to prove your ancestry - you simply need, as Peter proclaimed at Pentecost, to 'repent and be baptised'.

Speaker's Corner
The Best and Worst of the Church
Chick Yuill

What do you love most about the Church?
The odd, quirky, fascinating, frustrating variety of people who make up the Church!

What do you struggle with most about the Church?
The odd, quirky, fascinating, frustrating variety of people who make up the Church!

Workout
Assembly Time

Consider the following contexts in which the word 'assembly' is used in our culture:

» **A school assembly**

» **A political or legislative assembly**
(The Northern Ireland, Scottish and Welsh Assemblies; the London Assembly)

» **An assembly line**

» **The 'Auto Assembly'**
www.autoassembly.org.uk the world's largest convention for Transformers' fans

What do each of the groups involved in the assemblies above come together to do? How does this reflect an aspect of the Church? How is it different? How does picturing each of these give you insight into the 'assembly' that is the Church?

If you weren't allowed to use the words congregation, fellowship, assembly or church, what other words could you use to describe the corporate nature of 'ekklesia'?

9] Stanley J Grenz, *Theology for the Community of God*, Broadman and Holman, 1994
10] See for example Deuteronomy 23:1ff; 1 Chronicles 28:8
11] Stanley J Grenz, *Theology for the Community of God*, Broadman and Holman, 1994

PEOPLE OF PURPOSE

Missiologist Lesslie Newbigin - one of the most influential thinkers of the 20th Century on the nature and task of the Church - roots the ongoing mission of the Church in this same sense of continuity with Israel:

The whole core of biblical history is the story of the calling of a visible community to be God's own people, his royal priesthood on earth, the bearer of his light to the nations. Israel is, in one sense, simply one of the petty tribes of the Semitic world. But Israel - the same Israel - is also the people of God's own possession. In spite of all Israel's apostasy, Israel is his, for his gifts and calling are without repentance. This little tribe, and no other, is God's royal priesthood, his holy nation. And the same is true in the New Testament. There is an actual, visible, earthly company which is addressed as 'the people of God', the 'body of Christ'.[12]

In the New Testament context the Church is the community through whom God is now working to bless the nations of the earth. Theirs is not a passive or static calling but a dynamic invitation to co-operate with God in the healing of creation: to engage with the Trinity in a life-wide dance as purposeful as it is beautiful.

FLAVOURS AND COLOURS

The sense of the Church as a 'people movement' called to impact the world is captured in the climax of the Apostle Paul's ecclesial vision in his letter to the Ephesians. Paul declares that the coming together of the *ekklesia* is not an accident of history but the fulfillment of God's long-held plans - the new expression of what God has always purposed. Paul refers to a mystery long-hidden in the heart of God, but now made plain[13] and asserts that God's intent is that now '...through the Church, the manifold wisdom of God should be made known to the rulers and authorities in the heavenly realms...'.[14]

What God is doing *now* in forming and shaping the Church is an expression of what he has always intended, 'according to his eternal purposes'.[15] The plans of God revealed in Eden and on Sinai and reflected in the lives of Deborah and David and Isaiah and Malachi, are now poured into the Church. The Church is the new vehicle of God's mission in the world. How best can we grasp the magnitude of this statement? Perhaps by looking back to what God was doing in these ancient stories, and asking how those same purposes might now be embodied in the Church. We can look to:

» Adam and Eve in the garden, asked to rule benevolently over the created world; to bring out its fruitfulness; to image God in the world.

» Moses on Sinai, given laws to shape the hearts of the people so that they could in turn embody God's character.

» David called to form and shape a nation by being a king 'after God's own heart'.

» Elijah and Isaiah and Jeremiah calling the people back to intimacy and obedience.

» Jesus, on a dusty Galilean hillside, reminding the Jews that they are called, as God's people, to be 'salt and light'[16] to their world.

» Supremely, Jesus laying down his life as 'a ransom for many', demonstrating once and for all the true depth and breadth of God's love for humanity.

The Creator has always looked for people who through intimacy and obedience will reflect his character, to bring out 'the God-flavours' and 'the God-colours' of the world.[17] The New Testament speaks of what God wants to do *in* people, but also of what he longs to do *through* people. God's plan has always been to shine through people and since the life, death, resurrection and ascension of Jesus, the movement that makes God's shining possible is called 'Church'.

12] Lesslie Newbigin, *The Household of God*, SCM, 1953; Paternoster, 1998
13] Ephesians 3:3-5
14] Ephesians 3:10, NIV
15] Ephesians 3:11, NIV
16] Matthew 5:13,14
17] Matthew 5:13,14, The Message

Workout
Exercises to Explore

Matthew 5 calls God's people to be both 'salt' and 'light'. Consider the usefulness of these images by completing the following two sentences:

'If it wasn't for salt I couldn't…'

'If it wasn't for light I couldn't…'

For Paul, this call relates directly to the finished work of Christ. As beneficiaries of the work of the Cross, we do not declare what God *wants to do* for the world but what he *has done* in Christ. Our joy as the people of God is to look back to the triumph of Christ and forward to its ultimate fulfillment. Paul declares that in Christ, God has reconciled everything to himself, explicitly including 'everything in heaven and on earth'.[18] The call of the Church is to co-operate with God in making this known; to celebrate and declare that which God has done; to proclaim all the *unsearchable riches of Christ*.

So What?
Flavours of God

Picture the community or area in which your Church gathers or serves. Can you name six specific areas in which God wants to bring out his 'flavours' in the created world? What, for example, would justice taste like in your area? What would the flavour of mercy be? What about beauty, fruitfulness, faithfulness, compassion? If the Church was to bring out these flavours more, who would be the first to taste them?

BEAMS OF FAITH'S LIGHT

GRAHAM TOMLIN SAYS OF EPHESIANS 3:10

God wants to show off his wisdom and craft to the rest of the cosmos. God the divine artist wants to hold an exhibition of such beauty and power and wisdom that anyone who looks on, whether they come from earth or heaven, will be overcome with wonder and awe. It is to be a display of his 'manifold' (the word can be otherwise translated as 'varied' or 'variegated') wisdom.[19]

The picture is of God's wise character being broadcast to the world like water from a sprinkler or buckshot from a gun - or like light from a prism. It is through *each of us* and through *all of us* that God's wisdom will shine. The category Paul chooses to picture this prismatic image is not that of *truth* or *love*, both of which are acknowledged New Testament categories in mission. It is, rather, that of *wisdom*, long established in the biblical narrative as being the application of God's truth and character to the everyday concerns of human life. The wisdom tradition in scripture is about *how we live*. Ephesians 3:10, then, is about God's light and life, through his people, illuminating every part of life and culture. The great Dutch statesman Abraham Kuyper used this same, prismatic imagery in his call for a truly culture-wide Christian witness.

The believing community, gathered around word and sacrament, must radiate beams of faith's light into the realm of common grace - into education, art, science, politics, business, economics and the marketplace.[20]

18] Colossians 1:20, NLT
19] Graham Tomlin, *The Provocative Church*, SPCK, 2002 and 2004
20] John Bolt, *A Free Church, A Holy Nation: Abraham Kuyper's American Public Theology*, Eerdmans, 2001

Workout
Spectrum Race?

» *How quickly can you name the seven colours of prismatic light?*

» *How many other colours can you name in exactly 60 seconds? Write down as many as possible.*

» *Look at your list and imagine how long it might be if you had a whole day instead of one minute... what does this tell you about the light that God is shining through the Church?*

Grasping the creation-wide scope of the task God has given to his *ekklesia* will highlight a number of issues of genuine importance to the churches of our day:

» Firstly, the challenge of Church and Mission - connecting the Church with mission, and mission with the Church.

The Church is God's 'Plan A'. This is God's brilliant idea, to find a new way of shining through people; a way that is not de-railed by Adam's sin; that can move beyond the ethnic boundaries of Israel to touch every nation; that has such vast potential that in time the very 'rulers and authorities' of heaven will see the light. Recognising the Church as Plan A implies that the connection between the *Church* and *mission* is foundational. We are called *to* God so that we can shine for him.

» Secondly, the challenge of Church and kingdom - engaging with the breadth of God's mission in the world.

The things God wants to do in the Church are steps towards what God wants to do *through* the Church. The overwhelming love God has for us is a measure of his love for the whole world. The calling together of the Church is, from the very beginning, a step towards the blessing of the nations. The light of God will touch the whole created order when the mission of the Church is expressed both in its *gathering* and its *dispersal*: God's people carrying light to every corner of the world, honouring the God who gathers to send and sends to gather.

» Thirdly, the challenge of Equipping the Church - releasing God's people into their many and varied callings.

God is unswervingly and eternally committed to *working through people:* he has chosen to limit himself to that which is possible through human agency. Whatever God wants to achieve in the world, he will achieve through people. There is no plan B. God will shine through us, or not at all. Each of us has *vocations* and *callings* that give meaning and significance to our lives in the purposes of God. As Paul repeats over and over in Ephesians, God's mission is for *each* of us and *all* of us.

Speaker's Corner
The Best and Worst of the Church
Lisa Holmes

WHAT DO YOU LOVE ABOUT THE CHURCH? I LOVE THAT THE CHURCH IS A PLACE OF GREAT DIVERSITY BUT UNITED IN LOVE FOR JESUS AND EACH OTHER. I LOVE MY CHURCH FOR BEING WILLING TO TAKE RISKS; THAT IT'S PREPARED TO TRY AND FAIL RATHER THAN NOT TRY AT ALL. **WHAT DO YOU STRUGGLE WITH MOST ABOUT THE CHURCH?** I STRUGGLE WITH THE CHURCH WHEN WE LOSE SIGHT OF OUR REAL IDENTITY AND CALLING AND FIGHT OVER STUFF THAT REALLY DOESN'T MATTER TOO MUCH.

So What?
Models of the Church

The big questions Christians disagree about when it comes to ecclesiology – the 'What is it?' of the Church – are these:

1. Is the true Church visible (the institution you can see) or invisible (the company of faithful believers)?
2. Is the Church something that is in continuity with the apostles, or can it be reinvented throughout history?
3. Is the authority of the Church derived from its leader or leaders, or from the teachings of scripture?
4. Is the Church a human institution or a divine society?
5. Is the Church called to preach and teach an unchanging set of beliefs and doctrines, or can its teachings change and develop?
6. Is the Church called to be one institution, or are we to be 'spiritually' one in a number of denominations?
7. Must the Church have specially set apart ministers/bishops/priests/elders or can you still be the Church if you have no ordained leaders?

The ways in which we answer these questions will determine what sort of Church we believe in. But of course, it's not always either/or – it might well be both/and!

Avery Dulles, a Jesuit Cardinal, wrote a book called *Models of the Church* (1978) which sets out some of these issues. In simplified form, Dulles' models are:

Model	Who teaches it	According to this model, the Church is...	You can't have Church without...	Main emphases
Institution	Roman Catholics	Visible	Bishops and hierarchy	Tradition, History
Communion	Renewalists	Invisible	Holy Spirit	Fellowship, Relationship
Sacrament	Orthodox Orthodox	A sign of grace	Sacraments	Grace, Mystery
Herald	Evangelicals	God's vehicle of proclamation	Bible and gospel	Scripture, Evangelism
Servant	Radicals	God's servant	Justice and service	World, social concern

CHURCH AND MISSION

THE CHURCH IS AN EXPRESSION OF, AND A
VEHICLE FOR, GOD'S MISSION IN THE WORLD

The 'marrying' of the people of God to the mission of God has been one of the most significant developments of recent years in the fields of ecclesiology and missiology. As Western churches have woken up to the significant challenges of their post-Christendom context, a widespread move has taken place to move 'mission' to the very top of the Church's agenda. With this has come the recognition that mission is not simply a task of the Church but is fundamental to its nature. As has been said often, 'It is not the the Church of God has a mission, but that the mission of God has a Church.'

In recent years this has led to the widespread use of the term 'missional church' and to an explosion of tools and resources aimed at empowering God's people to become 'missional'. Alan Roxburgh, Fred Romanuk and Eddie Gibbs, three pioneer researchers in this area, have worked together to identify just what the 'missional church' is:

'God is about a big purpose for the whole of creation. The Church has been called into life to be both the means of this mission and a foretaste of where God is inviting all creation to go. Just as its Lord is a mission-shaped God, so the community of God's people exists, not for themselves but for the sake of the work. Mission is therefore not a programme or project some people in the Church do from time to time (as in 'mission trip', 'mission budget' and so on); the Church's very nature is to be God's missionary people. We use the word *missional* to mark this big difference. Mission is not about a project or a budget, or a one-off event somewhere; it's not even about sending missionaries. A missional Church is a community of God's people who live into the imagination that they are, by their very nature, God's missionary people living as a demonstration of what God plans to do in and for all of creation in Jesus Christ.'[21]

In the UK this has lead to the very significant report *Mission-Shaped Church* being published by the Anglican Church, under the chairmanship of Graham Cray, Bishop of Maidstone. In his foreword to the report Rowan Williams, Archbishop of Canterbury, urges flexibility and adaptability in the shape of the Church:

If 'Church' is what happens when people encounter the risen Jesus and commit themselves to sustaining and deepening that encounter in their encounter with each other, there is plenty of theological room for diversity of rhythm and style, so long as we have ways of identifying the same living Christ at the heart of every expression of Christian life in common.[22]

The report asserts the intimate connection of 'Church' with the mission of God, affirming the missional calling of God's people:

The Church is both the fruit of God's mission – those whom he has redeemed, and the agent of his mission – the community through whom he acts for the world's redemption. 'The mission of the Church is the gift of participating through the Holy Spirit in the Son's mission from the Father to the world.'[23]

Workout
What does mission mean?

The thesaurus offers the following words as possible substitutes for 'mission'. Put each of these in the place of mission in the phrase 'God's mission in the world'. How does this help you to grasp what 'mission' means in relation to the Church?

ASSIGNMENT   JOURNEY

EXPEDITION   TASK

COMMISSION

OPERATION   QUEST

PURPOSE   FUNCTION

UNDERTAKING

ALAN
HIRSCH

21] Alan Roxburgh Fred Romanuk, *The Missional Leader: Equipping Your Church to Reach a Changing World,* John Wiley & Sons, 2006
22] Rowan Williams, Archbishop of Canterbury, Foreword to *Mission Shaped Church,* Church House, 2004
23] James Torrance, *Worship, Community and the Triune God of Grace,* Paternoster, 1996, p. ix. cited in *Mission Shaped Church,* Church House 2004

The significance of 'mission-shaped Church' has been acknowledged beyond the boundaries of the Anglican denomination, and has led to widespread emergence of fresh expressions of Church, defined as:

'A form of Church for our changing culture established primarily for the benefit of people who are not yet members of any Church, which comes into being through principles of listening, service, incarnational mission and making disciples, and has the potential to become a mature expression of Church shaped by the gospel and the enduring marks of the Church and for its cultural context.'[24]

The Fresh Expressions movement is one among many responses to the challenges of missional Church, but is particularly significant in that it is an evolutionary rather than a revolutionary development. It is established, denominational churches that are engaging with the process, resulting in 'expressions' that are high in innovation, flexibility and risk. Fresh Expressions is demonstrating that it is possible for existing models and structures of the Church to adapt to changing times: that the journey into missional church allows for continuity as well as change.[25]

Alan Hirsch, a globally respected thinker on the Church and mission, asserts that the qualities and capacities that make mission possible - which he describes as forming the Church's 'missional DNA' - are present by definition in every Christian Church, even if they have fallen into disuse.

Imagine there was a power that lies hidden at the very heart of God's people. Suppose this power was built into the initiating 'stem cell' of the Church by the Holy Spirit but was somehow buried and lost through centuries of neglect and disuse. Imagine that if rediscovered, this hidden power could unleash remarkable energies that could propel the Church well into the twenty-second century - a missional equivalent to unlocking the power of the atom... I now believe that the idea of latent, inbuilt, missional potencies is not a mere fantasy; in fact there are primal forces that lie latent in every Jesus community and in every true believer... [26]

So What?
Hidden Power

Alan Hirsch suggests that the power of mission is locked into the Church like the power of the atom. Not that God needs to 'split' the Church to release its power, but that all the potential of the gospel is contained deep within the Church. Does this idea make sense to you? If you thought that there was 'atomic power' locked into your local church, where would you go to start looking for it?

In this analysis, the challenge to 'become' the missional Church is not so much a call for something new and unknown, as a call to rediscover and recover the roots of the Church: the very factors that have made the people of God what they are. Alison Morgan writes that:

'The gospel has been a force for change throughout history and all over the world, wherever and whenever it has been effectively preached and wholeheartedly embraced, both in the lives of individuals and through them to the societies of which they form part. And yet that is not the case, by and large, in the West today. There have been exceptions, but on the whole the last 300 years have been a period of decline, of loss of confidence in the power of the word, and of decreasing ability in the Church to proclaim it ...We must learn again to turn the word into a language, a living language that can speak into the assumptions of our culture just as Jesus spoke into the assumptions of his... '[27]

'Missional church' then is not a description of a new or currently non-existent church. It is rather, a label for the journey all our churches need to take, as they take seriously God's call to mission: placing mission at the heart of the Church and the Church at the heart of mission.

24] *Fresh Expressions Prospectus Volume 2*. Fresh Expressions
25] see http://www.youtube.com/watch?v=vKbFAcT16cM
26] Alan Hirsch, *The Forgotten Ways: Reactivating the missional church*, Brazos Press, 2006
27] Alison Morgan. *The Wild Gospel*, http://www.fulcrum-anglican.org.uk/page.cfm?ID=252

HOPEquotes:

Unconditional Service

'More doors have opened for Lancaster churches to work together alongside police and local authorities. Instead of expecting the community to join with our projects, we look for ways to contribute to community and council programmes. For us, being people of hope means being unconditional in our service yet unapologetic about our faith.'[28]

So What?

The Church and Mission

*The term 'Mission-Shaped Church' implies a simple but powerful idea - that the **form** or **shape** of the local church should be a reflection of God's mission in a given context. This throws up three key questions to explore in the local setting:*

» ***What shapes us?*** *What has given our particular church the shape it has? What are the factors and influences that dictate who we are and what we do? If these are **not** to do with God's mission in our world, how can we change them?*

» ***What is God's mission in our context?*** *What is there in your immediate area or further afield that God's wants to get done, and can get done through your expression of Church? What might God be able to tick-off his 'to-do' list as a result of your church's life and ministry?*

» ***What shape should that make us?*** *If you were to re-orientate the activities and patterns of your church around God's mission, what shape might that give? Would you still gather as you do now? What might your gatherings look like? Who would they be for? What else would you do, outside of your times of gathering?*

CHURCH AND KINGDOM

THE PURPOSE OF THE CHURCH IS TO BE USED BY GOD IN BRINGING HIS KINGDOM ON EARTH

If 'missional church' sets the Church at the heart of God's purposes for the world, it also recognises the breadth of those purposes - God is working *in* the Church and *through* the Church, but looking for an impact far *beyond* the boundaries of the Church. The 'reign of God' or 'kingdom of God' is about God's will being done throughout the created order in the Church but also in the other spheres of life and culture. This is the context in which the mission of the Church is set. Stanley Grenz writes that:

'If we were to point to one topic that above all others has been the recipient of the labours of biblical scholars and theologians in the 20th century it would no doubt be the kingdom of God. Indeed the idea of the divine reign, as depicting God's overall intention, lies at the heart of much of the Bible. It is not surprising, therefore, that the appearance of the Church in the New Testament era occurred within the context of the biblical teaching of the broader reality of God's rule. Consequently, our ecclesiology must set forth our understanding of the Church within the context of God's reign.'[29]

This touches on some of the most ancient beliefs of the Christian faith community. Veli-Matti Kärkkäinen, in his survey of ecclesiology through the years, points out that the Orthodox Church, the world's oldest surviving denomination, has always seen the witness of the Church in this wider context.

'At the very core of Orthodox theology in general and ecclesiology in particular, is the relation of humanity to creation as a whole, the cosmos. The Church is described in cosmological terms. In this understanding, the Church is the centre of the universe, the sphere in which its destinies are determined.'[30]

American author Rodney Clapp, in his influential 1996 book, *A Peculiar People*, makes a similar claim:

'The goal or proper end of human life, according to the Old Testament, is not the individual soul's flight from the constraints of time and body. It is instead the enjoyment of wholeness in communion with God and God's people, amid a healed and no longer strife-ridden creation. In this enduring Jewish tradition, the New Testament looks ahead to the communal resurrection of those redeemed in Christ (1 Corinthians 15) and longs for the healing of the 'whole creation' (Romans 8:18-30). For the earliest church, then, evangelism was not a matter of inviting individuals to recall what they somehow already knew. It was rather a matter of inviting them to become part of nothing less than a new humanity, reborn of the last Adam who was Jesus the Nazarene.'[31]

God's mission, then, is wider than the Church. Though the Church sits at its heart as the engine of mission, its goals or scope fall much more widely, taking in the whole breadth of human and even non-human culture. There is no limit to the 'where' of God's desire to shine through his people: every corner of the world is included. As missiologist Samuel Escobar has said, this challenges deeply our understanding of mission.

It is necessary to correct the tendency to base mission on a few selected texts from the New Testament. What has to be grasped is God's purpose for humankind as revealed in scripture, and the missionary thrust of the whole history of salvation. This will throw new light on the nature of mission.[32]

29] Stanley J Grenz, *Theology for the Community of God*, Broadman and Holman, 1994
30] Veli-Matti Kärkkäinen, *An Introduction to Ecclesiology: Ecumenical, Historical and Global Perspectives*, IVP, 2002
31] Rodney Clapp, *A Peculiar People: the Church as Culture in a Post-christian Society*, IVP, 1996
32] Samuel Escobar, *A Time for Mission: The Challenge for Global Christianity*, IVP, 2003, cited in David W Smith, *Against the Stream: Christianity and Mission in an Age of Globalisation*, IVP, 2003

Workout
Kingdom Come

Bible translators have used a number of terms to capture the meaning of God's kingdom. These include:

» *The reign of God; (Young's Literal)*
» *God's way of doing and being right (Amplified);*
» *God's work (CEV);*
» *God-reality, God-initiative, God-provisions (The Message);*
» *God's Holy Nation (New Life Version)*

How do these different translations help you to understand what God's will is for your local community?

What does it mean for the Church to help bring this about?

GOD IN THE EVERYDAY

If the language of the Church has encouraged us to emphasise the importance of the things we do together, gathered as the people of God, then perhaps the language of kingdom can help us to value the things we do in the everyday. 'Kingdom' is about the places and settings in which we spend most of our time: our homes and schools and workplaces; our shopping centres and cinemas; our offices and studios and laboratories. Kingdom addresses the Houses of Parliament and the houses on your street. It is about what we eat and what we read; what we buy and watch and talk about. God's desire, Paul asserts, is for his wisdom to shine in all these places, and it is through his people that he intends for his wisdom to shine.

The definition of mission, in this light, is best captured not in the 'Great Commission' of Matthew 28, but in the Great Prayer of Matthew 5:

'Your kingdom come, your will be done, on earth as in heaven'

Wherever the will of God is *not* done on earth, there is scope for mission. Wherever the will of God *is* done where it was not before, mission has in some sense taken place since the mission of God is for the will of God to be done. Wherever God leads his people to work and pray for his will to be done, the missional church is at work. A helpful measure of the scope of God's mission has been the identification of the different 'spheres' of society and culture, sometimes referred to as the 'seven mountains' of culture. Any list of such spheres is by definition a simplification, but knowing that even these seven are on God's agenda for influence and transformation is a positive move towards a wider view of mission. The 'seven mountains' often acknowledged by missiologists are *business, government, media, arts and entertainment, education, the family and religion.*[33]

To these can be added the vital spheres of science and technology, by which so much of contemporary culture is shaped. A kingdom-oriented view of mission seeks the purposes of God for the whole of life and culture, asking how his people can bring the influence and impact he longs for in their spheres of influence. This might include the 'solo witness' of an individual, forging a lone path in a setting in which no other believers are involved, or it might involve believers working together to create kingdom structures and expressions of kingdom life in ever new areas. Deep biblical concern for justice, for example, might motivate change in the spheres of business (trade) and government, while a passion for truth brings transformation to the media and a love for beauty energises the arts. A longing to disciple the rising generations can lead to engagement in Sunday school and youth group activities, but it can also lead to long-term service in public education. Those engaged full-time in raising children can seek God's anointing on their missional actions, bringing the light of God not only to their own children but to other families as they grow together. Mark Roques and Jim Tickner's stimulating book *Fields of God* [34] takes the world of sport - specifically football - and asks where the mission of God and a kingdom orientation impacts this sphere. Their question is simple: if even football is included in the scope of God's kingdom, what could possibly be excluded? 'There is nothing so secular that it cannot be sacred.' [35]

Mark Roques offers an illustration of the difference that a kingdom-orientation or life-wide vision might make to our understanding of the Church and mission:

'At an international conference of church leaders, the convener asked the assembled participants what was the greatest problem in their countries. Almost all included bribery and corruption, often as the most serious problem they faced. The convener responded as follows: 'If corruption is the major problem, then why are we preparing our young people only to be pastors and evangelists? Why aren't we training them to be the godly entrepreneurs, economists, policemen, judges and politicians that our countries so desperately need?' [36]

33] http://www.reclaim7mountains.com/
34] Mark Roques and Jim Tickner, Fields of God: Football and the Kingdom of God, Authentic, 2003
35] Madeleine L'Engle, 'Walking on Water,' cited in Eddie Gibbs and Ryan K Bolger, Emerging Churches: Creating Christian Community in Postmodern Cultures, Baker Academic, 2005
36] Mark Roques and Arthur Jones, Culture Shapers, Reality Bytes, www.realitybites.org.uk

Workout
What are you praying for?

Mark Roques' example of praying for honest politicians gives a new perspective on Jesus' words in Matthew 9:36-38, 'When he saw the crowds, he had compassion on them because they were confused and helpless, like sheep without a shepherd. He said to his disciples,"The harvest is great, but the workers are few. So pray to the Lord who is in charge of the harvest; ask him to send more workers into his fields."'
Assuming the God's 'work' is the kingdom, and the field is your local community, what other kinds of workers might you pray for?

Mark Greene, Executive Director of the London Institute for Contemporary Christianity, diagnoses our short-sightedness as a case of 'SSD' (the 'sacred-secular divide'):

SSD is the pervasive belief that life is an orange not a peach, that some segments of our life are really important to God - prayer, church services, church-based activities - but that others aren't - work, school, university, sport, the arts, music, rest, sleep, hobbies. SSD is like a virus. It pervades the Church and pretty much everyone I know has had it and is a carrier. [37]

The cure, he suggests, is the recovery of 'whole-life discipleship', in which God's people discover and live out their missional callings in every sphere into which God leads them. A whole-life perspective, he writes:

'... enables us to see that every context we find ourselves in is not just a place to display Christian character - to model the ways of Jesus - but also a place to minister to others, to be a mouthpiece for truth and justice and the gospel, to be a maker of disciples and to be a maker of culture - a shaper of the way things are done. After all, a Christian secretary in an office may have the opportunity to 'pastor' more people in a day than a pastor; a doctor may have more opportunities to offer wisdom and comfort to those in suffering than a vicar; a 14-year-old at school may have more opportunities to share Jesus in a day than a church-paid youth evangelist.' [38]

Even that which we do *in* church, as the gathered people of God, will be changed by a life-wide view of God's mission. Jonny Baker has suggested just such a change in our understanding of our most valued 'gathered' activity, worship:

'God is encountered in the stuff of everyday life, not outside it. So worship makes two moves: it brings the real world into church, and it enables God to be encountered back in the real world. This is a direct challenge to an experience of the Church as a world apart, unrelated to the rest of life.' [39]

Crucial to the embracing of a 'prismatic' understanding of the Church is the recognition that the people of God have both a 'gathered' and a 'scattered' expression. We are Church when we come together to worship; to learn and grow and build one another up, but we are also Church when we disperse, carrying God's light into all the different places he takes us. Can we take seriously the question: 'what would it look like if the very nature of Church (our worship, our understanding of discipleship, our expression of community) were organised around God's mission in the world? Can our gathered expressions of Church truly fuel our missional dispersion?

37] Mark Greene, *The Great Divide*, LICC, 2010
38] Mark Greene, *The Great Divide*, LICC, 2010
39] Jonny Baker, cited in Eddie Gibbs and Ryan K Bolger, *Emerging Churches: Creating Christian Community in Postmodern Cultures*, Baker Academic, 2005

So What?
Mapping the Kingdom

There are two kinds of map that often turn up on the walls of churches. The first is a world map with little dots in far-flung places. Beside it will often be a label saying 'The missionaries we support'. The second is a local map, showing the area served by the Church: the town, or village or neighbourhood in which the Church's building is set.

Both of these maps represent aspects of the Church's kingdom footprint. But neither gives the whole picture.

What would happen if you created a third map, showing the 'locations of influence' of Church members? It might show, for starters:

» Where people live
» Where they work
» Where they serve as volunteers
» Where they belong to clubs and associations
» Where they study or teach

Such a map would include both those discussed above, but would be, overall, much bigger than the second. It would show you several things:

1. The incredible spread of the kingdom influence generated by just one congregation or gathering.

2. The significant 'clustering' of that influence. You might notice, for instance, a concentration of influence in a local school or hospital, or a particular housing development.

3. The huge diversity of influence represented by the body of the Church. A gathering of just 100 people will have influence on hundreds of different settings in many different contexts and, by implication, on thousands of people.

4. The local, regional, national and global connections your Church has.

Given such a map, you might begin a journey of prayer that asks 'What does God want to do with this influence?'. Where are the places of emphasis or concentration? What special ministries is God calling this particular group of people to take on? Who is isolated and in need of support? Who has opportunity but needs resourcing?

We might even learn, in time, to refer to this map when someone asks the innocent question, 'Where is your Church?'

HOPEquotes:

COFFEE AND SWEETS

"POLICE REQUESTED A COFFEE VAN FOR GLASTONBURY FOLLOWING SUCCESS OF ONE RUN BY FROME CHURCHES, REDUCING ANTI-SOCIAL BEHAVIOUR - WE LISTEN, SHARE AND CHAT WITH LATE NIGHT REVELLERS, GIVING AWAY COFFEE AND SWEETS. FOR US, BEING PEOPLE OF HOPE MEANS WE PROMOTE COMMUNITY SAFETY, MAKE OURSELVES AVAILABLE AND SHARE LIFE"[40]

40] Sam Brinn, HOPE Frome, Somerset

KINGDOM STRUCTURES BEYOND THE CHURCH

Mark Roques

The Story

The Neema Crafts Centre was set up by Yorkshire woman Susie Hart in 2003 in Tanzania. Ten percent of the population have severe disabilities and a survey found that the majority of disabled people lived in extreme poverty and due to the stigma of their disability suffered a lot of prejudice and discrimination.

The project began with three deaf men being taught in one room by Susie Hart who is also partially disabled. The deaf men were trained to turn elephant poo into paper. And they were also taught the skills of making handicrafts.

Today the centre employs 123 deaf and disabled people. They even have a football team made up of deaf people. Consider the following vignette of redemption, healing and restoration.

Hezron was a young man in his mid 20s with everything to live for - a lovely wife and two beautiful children - when the minibus taxi he was travelling in hit an oncoming car. All 30 people in the vehicle died, except for Hezron and a new born baby. Hezron lost the use of both legs and found himself wheelchair-bound at home, unable to support himself or his family. After two years of watching his wife and young children have to fend for themselves, he felt utterly worthless and was on the brink of suicide.

When he was first pushed to the Neema Craft Centre to ask for work his voice was barely audible, his self-esteem had sunk so low. He was taken on as a trainee weaver and today - one year on - he is full of life and enthusiasm. He has become a highly skilled weaver, enjoying the therapeutic activity involved and taking great pride in the beautiful items he produces. He peddles himself to work each day on the hand-pedal three-wheeler provided by the centre, and feels proud of himself and his ability to support his young family.

The joy he has found is plain for all to see by the broad smile he wears as he races his fellow weavers up the hill to work each morning.

Isn't this wonderful?

The Significance of the Story

This story is very significant when we think about the kingdom of God and the Body of Christ. Neema Crafts is not a Church! It is a redeemed business. Of course it is inspired and nurtured by Christian teaching, faith and wisdom but a business has a different calling from a local church. This redeemed kingdom structure was able to transform Hezron's life in a way that a local church cannot.

When Christians gather together as a local church they are not expected to make and produce handicrafts. There are many churches in Tanzania which do a great job. We affirm the vibrant worship and witness that these churches bring, but Neema is serving another purpose. Another calling. We should not attack the Neema Craft business by pointing out that it isn't a church! We should rejoice that a 'kingdom structure' beyond the boundaries of the local church can compliment the work of the local church. At the same time we should not attack a vibrant local church for failing to provide redemptive work opportunities for deaf and disabled people.

Exactly the same can be said with respect to George Cadbury's chocolate factory, Bob Lavelle's Christian bank and the Salvation Army model match factory.

When we reduce God's kingdom to the 'institutional' Church we will inevitably condemn culture to the tensions and miseries of secularisation. Hidden worldview stories indoctrinate us as Christians retreat into the Church sphere.

the idea of low interest savings banks to India, to fight the all-pervasive evil of usury, and he campaigned for the humane treatment of lepers. He struggled against human sacrifice and prevented the murder of many innocent children. Carey founded India's Agri-Horticultural Society in the 1820s, 30 years before the Royal Agricultural Society was established in England. He wrote some of the earliest essays on forest management and conservation. He wrote concerning this – 'If the gospel flourishes in India, the wilderness will, in every respect, become a fruitful field.'

And Carey was also a great preacher and evangelist! Carey affirmed and encouraged church activity and church attendance but he realised that the kingdom of God goes way beyond local church activity. He set up appropriate kingdom structures in different spheres of life and culture.

Can we, as local churches, work with vibrant non-ecclesiastical kingdom structures to transform culture and re-shape our communities?

Mark Roques, Reality Bytes

www.realitybites.org.uk

Workout
Kingdom Projects

*Mark Roques describes 'redeemed' and 'non-ecclesial' kingdom structures. In layman's terms, these are projects that Christians work on together to bring more of the kingdom, but that are explicitly **not** churches. What examples can you name of such projects in your area? What others can you imagine? If more existed, what would the role of local churches be in supporting them? If there are few you can name, why do you think this is so?*

THE EQUIPPING CHURCH

THE CHURCH FULFILS GOD'S MISSION BY EQUIPPING EACH AND ALL OF GOD'S PEOPLE FOR LIFE.

The recovery of a 'prismatic' understanding of the missional church requires a significant investment in the callings and vocations of ordinary people. *Vocation* is a word that has fallen out of use in many churches, or is restricted to those pursuing a full-time 'religious' career, but at heart it is for all God's people. It is rooted in the Latin 'to call', and simply describes the activities that we pursue in response to the call of God, whether these are expressed in job and career choices or in commitments made outside of paid employment. Frederick Buechner is credited with the most widely-known definition of vocation:

The place God calls you to is the place where your deep gladness and the world's deep hunger meet. [41]

Psychologist and theologian John Neafsey, who has dedicated himself to the study and exploration of vocation, offers a more detailed definition:

'People commonly associate vocation either with the call to ordained ministry or vowed religious life or with the popular secular understanding of vocation as being synonymous with a job, occupation or career. These are valid, but incomplete, understandings of vocation. Some people do have special callings to priesthood or ministry or religious life, but most don't. This does not mean that these others don't have a vocation, but rather that God has another purpose in mind for them, something else for them to do or be. Similarly, though the kind of work we do is an important dimension of our calling, it is important not to define the rich, complex phenomenon of vocation too narrowly or exclusively in terms of job or profession ... Vocation potentially touches and encompasses *every* level and dimension of our lives. This includes our family life, our love life, our creative interests and pursuits, and our politics. Basically *anything* we do with our time and talents and resources can be infused with a sense of vocation.' [42]

Vocation is not another word for 'work' or 'job' - it does not simply describe what you do to earn a living, even though it is often used in that context. Rather, it is the original word for 'calling' - it describes what you do to surrender your gifts and energies to the purposes of God. Our primary or fundamental vocation is discipleship - we are called to follow Christ. But out of this will flow, for each of us, more specific callings: particular ways in which, in particular places and contexts, we can obey God, express his character and wisdom and so bring him glory.

Many contemporary missiologists insist that the mission of the Church *depends* on the recovery of vocation - ordinary people finding, in the call of an extraordinary God, the keys to fruitfulness.

'We are to be the billboards of the gospel in the extraordinary ordinariness of our daily lives - extraordinary because of the renewing power of the Holy Spirit, ordinary because of the common creational stuff of our daily existence. It is in that profoundly this-worldly and mundane sense that creation, to use Calvin's arresting phrase, is the theatre of God's glory.' [43]

AL WOLTER WRITES

41] Frederick Buechner cited in John Neafsey, *A Sacred Voice is Calling:Personal Vocation and Social Conscience,* Orbis, 2006
42] John Neafsey, *A Sacred Voice is Calling:Personal Vocation and Social Conscience*, Orbis, 2006
43] Al Wolters, *Creation* in *Comment Magazine*, March 2010 http://www.cardus.ca/comment/article/2022/

Workout
Life on Mars

A visiting Martian has asked you to show him some sights and locations that demonstrate the meaning of your Christian faith. Unfortunately, his visit to Planet Earth does not include a weekend. What can you show him?

Alan Hirsch and Lance Ford have taken up this challenge in the first of a series of resources produced for the *Shapevine* [44] movement. They write that:

It is absolutely critical that we as the whole people of God are activated. If missional church remains solely in the domain of leaders and clergy, then it is doubtful we will have any lasting missional impact in the long term. It's going to take both *missional church plus missional disciples to make a missional movement.* [45]

Workout
Calling all Christians

How many people are members or regular attenders of your local Church? Of these, how many would you think of as having a clear sense of God's calling on their lives: they know what God has called them to do, and where, and are working to develop the gifts and resources they need to do it. Express the number you think this is as a percentage of the whole. If this is a low percentage, what would it take to make it higher? What would the pattern of your Church's meetings / services look like if it was close to 100%?

44] www.shapevine.com
45] Alan Hirsch and Lance Ford, *Right Here Right Now: Everyday Mission for Everyday People*, Baker Books, 2011

LISTENING PATHWAYS

Such a movement will require a committed process of listening - to discern the callings and vocations that God is already speaking to his people. Alan Roxborough and M Scott Boren write:

'We propose a way of listening to the imagination the Spirit is giving ordinary people in local churches. This is where we discover the missional pathways the Spirit is birthing in our time. We want to emphasise that it's a movement of ordinary people in ordinary churches, because this is where the Spirit is at work gestating and birthing a new movement of God. The releasing of the missional imagination of God's people in the midst of the ordinary and everyday is far more powerful and transforming than importing a predetermined plan from the outside.' [46]

Beyond simply identifying the callings of all God's people, the role of the Church is to *equip* them for their fulfillment. In Ephesians 4:12, Paul insists that all the leadership roles established in the Church exist for the same core purpose: to equip God's people. Disciple-making, the central activity of the church, goes beyond personal-faith growth into the whole realm of equipping - discerning, developing and deploying the gifts God has given to his people. A working definition of 'prismatic' mission might be:

ALL THE COLOURS OF GOD'S WISDOM
THROUGH ALL THE CALLINGS OF GOD'S PEOPLE
TO EVERY CORNER OF GOD'S WORLD

Workout
Mission as a Mirror Ball

One image that attempts to capture the 'gathered' and 'scattered' dimensions of the Church and the kingdom is the image of a mirror ball. The central, organised and highly structured ball serves to 'throw out' light in tiny, scattered pieces.
Can you apply this image to your Church? If you wanted your local church to embrace a 'mirror ball' mission, what steps would you need to take?

EQUIPPING IS THE KEY

At the heart of this process is equipping: building up God's people until each one has the resources needed for fruitfulness in their everyday arenas. There is more to say of this, and our exploration of what it means to be the 'Community of the Spirit' will explore further, but it suffices here to say that what makes the Church central to God's creation-wide mission is it's function as an engine of equipping. This calls for a new approach to leadership, according to Bill Easum and Bill Tenny-Brittian. A prismatic culture in the Church requires leaders who function

'... like gardeners. their role is to create a nurturing environment in which people are welcomed, transformed, equipped and empowered to do God's will rather that fulfill the needs of the institutional Church.'[47]

The emphasis on leadership as 'equipping' will impact how we view both ordained and lay leadership: both the functioning of full-time leaders and of occasional volunteers. At every level, 'equipping' provides a central paradigm of what leadership means in the Church. Whatever structures of leadership and ordination a church adopts, it is our shared responsibility, as God's people, to work and pray for the equipping of *all*.

46] Alan J Roxburgh and M Scott Boren, *Introducing the Missional Church: What it is, Why it Matters, How to Become One,* Baker Books, 2009
47] Bill Easum and Bill Tenny-Brittian, *Under the Radar: Learning from Risk-Taking Churches,* Abingdon, 2005

Workout
Mending Nets, Setting Bones

Paul's word for 'equipping' God's people in Ephesians 4:12 is the same word used in Matthew 4:21 when John and James are seen mending their fishing nets. Elsewhere in Greek literature, it is used of re-setting broken bones. What does this say to you about the role of the Church to equip God's people for their callings in the world?

MOVEMENT NOT MAINTENANCE

To come full-circle to the beginning of our exploration of the Church, such an approach to vocation re-establishes the essential nature of the Church as a movement of people sharing missional goals and equipping one another to fulfill them. This, suggests Alan Hirsch, is the key to our future mission:

'I believe with all my heart that the future of Christianity in the West is somehow bound up with the idea of becoming a people *movement* once again.' [48]

IN HERE – OUT THERE

The description of the Church as a *people movement* militates against the static or fixed nature of the Church as many of us have experienced it. *Moving* is the last thing many of the people in our churches seem to be doing. What will it take for the churches of our day to be described, honestly and authentically, as a people movement?

Neil Hudson reminds us of the challenge facing every kind of church:

'There have been a range of innovative approaches to Church over the past decade or so. Many people have set out to re-think what we mean by Church. They have experimented with new forms of existing Church, new forms of Church planting and new forms of Church for the de-churched, the un-churched, the never-thought-about-it-churched. However, whatever form the Church takes, however different people come to belong to the community, they will all face the same central issue;

how do we ensure that our life together equips us for our life when we are separated from one another; how do we make whole-life disciples?
So it doesn't matter if you are:
a traditional church, a middle of the road church, or a new church;
» a fresh expression, a mission-shaped community, or a new monastic
» a cathedral, a community or a chapel
» a preaching centre, a worship centre or a prayer centre; Soul Survivor, Keswick or Walsingham
» post-evangelical, post-charismatic or neo-reformed; urban, suburban or rural...
Wherever you fit in the spectrum, the challenge remains: how does what we do 'in here' enable people to live for Christ 'out there'. [49]

Workout
In Here, Out There

Neil Hudson's model of churches where the 'in-here' resources the 'out there' begs a question. If the whole Church is focused on resourcing the kingdom, who resources the Church? Looking back at Ephesians 4:11-13, what is Paul's answer to this problem? Can you see how a model built on vocations-for-all can result in a strong Church and a vibrant kingdom?

Speaker's Corner
The Best and Worst of the Church
Norman Ivison

What do you love most about the Church?
The fact that increasingly the church is trying new things and moving from a 'come to us and become like us' model to a 'we'll come to you and stay with you' way of being. That seems much more like Jesus.

What do you struggle with most about the Church?
The fact that so many people find it culturally irrelevant and so difficult to belong to.

48] Alan Hirsch in Alan Hirsch and Lance Ford, *Right Here Right Now: Everyday Mission for Everyday People*, Baker Books, 2011
49] Neil Hudson, *Imagine Church Releasing Whole-Life Disciples*, IVP, 2012

RIGHT WHERE YOU ARE?

Mark Greene

Our primary calling as Christians is to be disciples of Jesus... and that vocation can, and should be expressed in any location. Still, in our work at LICC, we've found that one of the hardest things for many Christians to really believe is that the places we already spend time – at home, at work, in the mall, in the gym – might actually, really be our mission field... the place where God can use us to be a blessing, to do good work in the power of the Spirit, to bring wisdom, love, truth, justice, to be a mouthpiece for the gospel. However, once people are affirmed in the location of their vocation... well, everything begins to change.

Isabelle, a grandmother, hadn't seen that the regular conversations she was having with her 23 year old non-believing granddaughter over Sunday lunch about the church service and the sermon meant that she really did have a mission field... **but** when she did, her confidence soared. God was already using her! Her home group began to support her in prayer and her vicar began to think of things to say in the sermon that would help Isabelle later over lunch...

Ed, a factory worker, couldn't see that his factory might be the place where God wanted him to make a kingdom contribution... **but** when he realised that his calling was to be an agent of blessing there, it transformed his attitude and he began to engage with his co-workers and pray for them and pray with them...

Sheona, a headmistress who'd successfully turned round two schools, hadn't seen that the wonderful impact she'd had on hundreds of kids and parents and scores of staff was really kingdom work... **but** when she did, it didn't change what she did, but it gave her a new confidence, a new joy – God was already using her where she was...

Now, this understanding that the God of the whole earth might want to work through his people in any location, is a profound challenge to the way we do church together. It will impact how we view the call of mission, which for many churches could currently be summarised as:

To recruit the people of God to use some of their leisure time to join the missionary initiatives of church-paid workers.

Certainly, God has used his people wonderfully through this model – among the poor, among mums and toddlers, among drug addicts and the homeless and late-night clubbers, among prisoners and latch-key kids, among the lonely and the housebound... Praise God for that. And there's no reason to stop it. But what would happen if our model of mission broadened to releasethe whole people of God into mission, not just in the five to ten hours we can give in our leisure time but in all of our time but where we already have relationships, where we are already making a contribution? And what would happen if we recognised that we are members of Jesus' body; that we are the Church, actually, just as much when we are separated from each other out in the world as we are when we are worshipping together in the sanctuary or ministering together in a home group? In sum, what would happen if we understood that our calling is to be disciples of Jesus in all of life? And that we as Church communities are there to help each other do that? What would happen?

We'd all know the humbling, liberating, sobering joy of realising that the King of the Universe has a purpose for us in his mission.

And our nation would hear and see the gospel.

Mark Greene
Executive Director of the London Institute for Contemporary Christianity

www.licc.org/imagine

So What?
Equipping the Equippers

The journey from where many of us are right now to the full realisation of an equipping Church may be long and sometimes painful. But there are several steps we can take to begin in any given setting.

*1. **Reflection.** We can begin to reflect on what an equipping Church might look like in our context. This can simply begin with the questions of who, what, when and how:*
  » ***Who** do we have in our ekklesia?*
  » ***What** is God calling them to do in serving him?*
  » ***Where** are they serving?*
  » ***How** might the Church more fully equip them for this service?*

*2. **Prayer.** We can bring the results of our reflections to God in prayer, and begin to pray for the changes we need to see. If we need resources, inspiration, leadership, time and space for this change, let's ask God to open-up these things to us.*

*3. **Conversation.** Never underestimate the power of conversation. In Malachi 3:16 we are told that 'Those who feared the Lord spoke with each other, and the Lord listened to what they said.' Sometimes a movement of change begins when someone simply says 'Is anyone else feeling what I'm feeling?'*

HOW TO BECOME A WHOLE-LIFE DISCIPLE-MAKING CHURCH

Mark Greene suggests ten things you can do to re-shape your local church around life-wide mission

1 **Release the vision... rooted it in the whole-life gospel...** it's Jesus-following, it's Cross-shaped, it's Spirit-empowered, it's central, it's missional, it's liberating. It's for everyone and it needs everyone – cleaners and accountants, builders and barristers, 7 year olds and 77 year olds. It's for out there as well as in here. It's for others as well as us. It takes a long time and it's hard... it's a revolution. It's truly loving. And it's urgent.

2 **Create a new community conversation** – help each other express it and imagine its implications and challenges together – whatever gets everyone talking to everyone...

3 **Start small but strategic** – let the yeast get to work, help the Church identify and initiate one degree shifts, Trojan mice, mustard seeds that carry the new DNA...

6 **Focus on the frontline** – this isn't about making the Church run more smoothly but helping God's people be more fruitful... You'll know you're succeeding when people tell the stories of what's going on out there in your daily lives... wherever that frontline is – the local supermarket, the school gate, the office, the club...

7 **Celebrate success stories** – frontline testimonies (FTs). No FT, no progress. Make sure people are listening for them and recording them and make sure they are told in a way that connects clearly to whole-life principles. These are stories about God at work – wonderful fuel for praise in prayer and worship...

8 **Expand the pastor/people contract** – from purely pastoral care to pastoral equipping for all of life. This isn't just about the 'leader' adding pastoral equipping to their role, it's about the whole community recognising the kind of people you are there to help one another become...

4 **Find and empower the championing team** – the SWAT team who really, really want to make this happen. Make sure there are lay and church-paid members...

5 **Cultivate a biblical imagination** – teach, preach, pray, chat with the aim of developing a gospel-shaped, whole-life, Spirit-filled, biblical imagination...

9 **Love one another. Crawl, stumble, walk in grace and in step with the Spirit** – whole-life discipleship must not become a new version of salvation by works; a whole set of hurdles to jump; a whole new way to feel inadequate and guilty. So cheer one another on. You're all learning to change – and God is your gracious Father, not a finger-wagging, grumpy old headmaster.

10 **Never surrender** – fight for the whole-life, gospel life in prayer, fight for it in Bible study, fight for it in song choice, fight for it in home groups, fight for it in bulletins and announcements and web communications, fight for it in business meetings and training programmes and budget allocation. Never surrender your life-wide vision for the Church.

www.licc.org.uk/imagine

TAKE SPRING HARVEST HOME... TAKEAWAYS FROM HOPE

In this session we have seen something of the wonder of what the Church really is and its missional purpose. We have been reminded that the gospel has been a force for change throughout history. We have also seen that this is a people movement, that this force is carried in the lives of God's people.

This truth which has been brought to us again has come to the Church many times but has not achieved the impact that we hoped. A number of years ago Laurence Singlehurst, a writer of books on mission, had an experience where he realised that many of these missional endeavours and people movements were in fact just another programme. They worked as long as leaders pushed and God spoke to him saying 'being missional isn't a programme, it is a question and the question is 'How big is your heart?''

So how big is your heart? And how do we get a big heart so that every Christian is motivated from the inside to be missional? There are three steps:

» Firstly, 2 Corinthians 5:14 says that 'the love of Christ controls us because we are convinced that one has died for all'. The death of Christ has revalued every human being, whether black or white, rich or poor, clean or dirty, they all have the same value. The first step in being big hearted is to see value in every human being.
» Secondly, 2 Corinthians 5:16 says 'from now on, therefore, we regard no one from a human point of view'. So to be big hearted we must look beyond what we see in terms of class or background, colour or race, and look, as God looks, to that inner value.
» Thirdly, these verses affirm that Christ died for all. Jesus made a choice to be motivated by love. So, for us, love for others begins in our hearts, changes our values and expresses itself through our choices.

So our Takeaway is, let's not be pushed into mission, or try to love by obligation, but let's ask God for a big heart and to see people the way he sees them.

Laurence Singlehurst and Roy Crowne, HOPE, www.hopetogether.org.uk

CELEBRATE GOD'S BRILLIANT IDEA

At the heart of this session of the *Theme Guide* has been the acknowledgment of God's desire to *let them shine.* The Church, in this view, is the people-movement through which the Creator is seeking to bless his creation. What can we celebrate about this remarkable idea?

(1) We can rejoice that God thinks enough of people to want to be in communion with us. God loves people. He's crazy about us. He has done everything possible to make us part of his purposes for the world.

(2) We can celebrate the astounding ways in which the Church has, over centuries, shone with God's brilliant light.

(3) We can celebrate the thousands of ways in which God's Church, today, shines his light in communities across the world, offering hope and joy.

(4) We can each celebrate the joy and love we have found in the company of God's people.

(5) Perhaps above all, we can celebrate God's unflinching commitment to this idea: his determination to shine through us. In the words of Paul to his friends in the church in Philippi, we can rejoice that God is so determined to bring to completion the work he has begun in us:

And I am certain that God, who began the good work within you, will continue his work until it is finally finished on the day when Christ Jesus returns [50]

Speaker's Corner
The Best and Worst of the Church
Anon

What do you love most about the Church?
I really love and appreciate many of the people who attend church. I also really admire the great work the Church does with asylum seekers and the homeless.

What do you struggle with most about the Church?
I struggle with the dualism in the Church. This is the sacred/secular split. Church life and its busy programmes are overvalued, and the callings of those 'outside' the Church are devalued. I also struggle with some of the worship songs which can be trite and otherworldly.

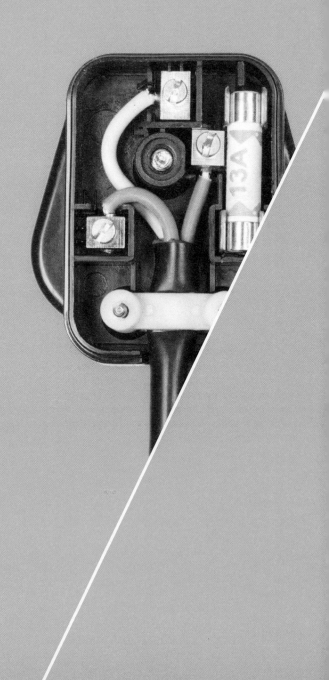

2.
give
them
power

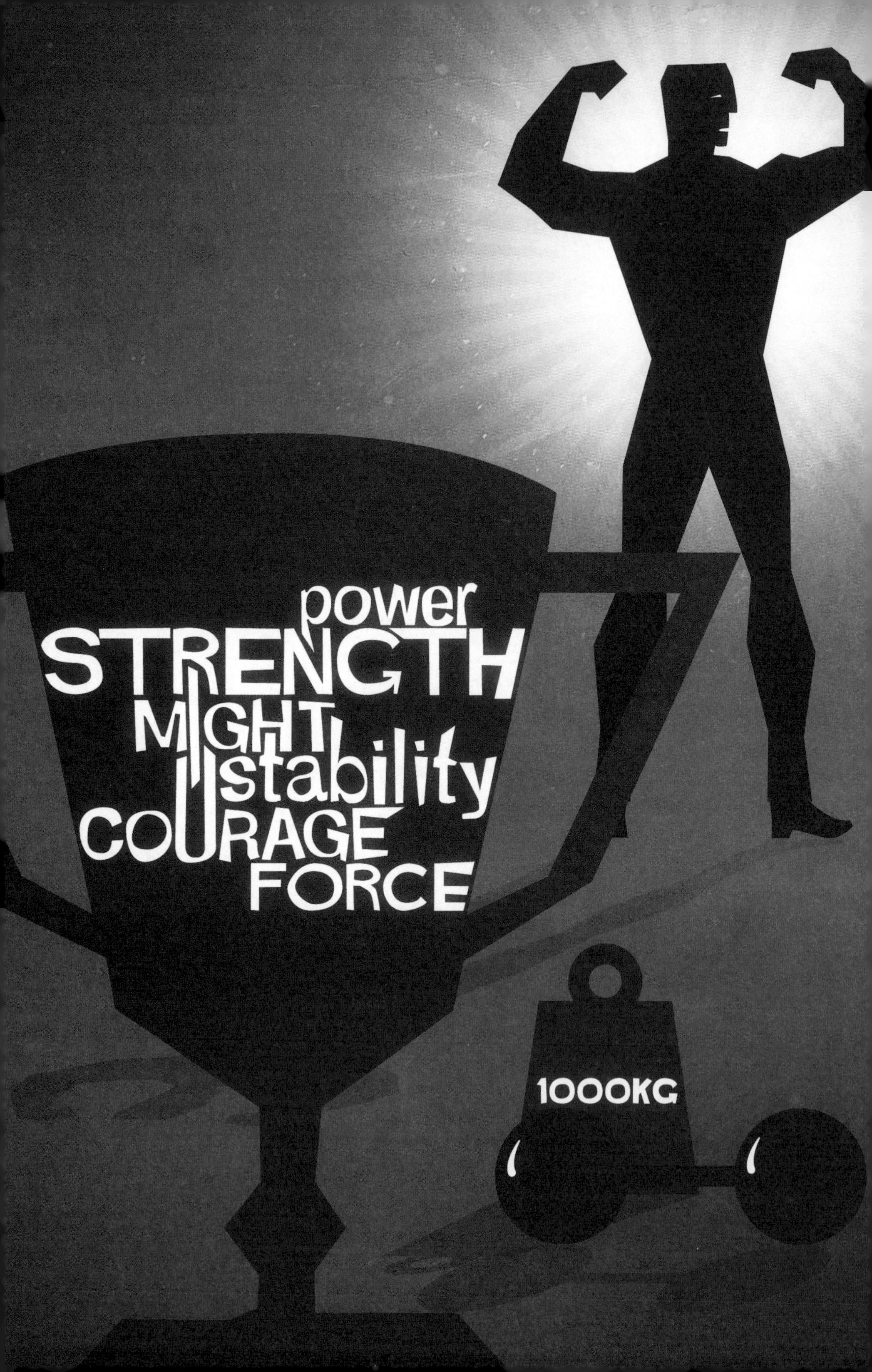
power
STRENGTH
MIGHT stability
COURAGE
FORCE
1000KG

give them power

THE CHURCH AS THE COMMUNITY OF THE SPIRIT

The brilliant thing about God's plan for the Church is that he has never asked us to make it on our own. He doesn't expect us to come up with the ideas and the energy to change the world. Instead, he offers us his resources: an unlimited source of power; a battery that never runs out. God does not simply call us to be his people and leave us to it - he gives us fuel for the journey; he travels with us; he pours out all the resources we need; he shapes us to be the people he is calling us to be.

The Church is the community of the Spirit. It is a community in which God himself dwells. He does not only offer us his gifts - he offers us himself. There is nothing God will ever ask me to do for which he will not also empower me. There is no task to which he will call me for which he will not also equip me. God does not wait until we are qualified to call us: he calls us, then trains us, just as he trained the first disciples. We are first called, and then equipped. He has what we need, to be what he wants us to be.

Being shaped by God's presence. Being fuelled by his power. Being formed for his purposes. These are the adventures God calls us to in his Church. If we will accept his invitation, we will never be the same again - and neither will our world.

WHAT WILL WE DISCOVER IN THIS *CHURCH ACTUALLY* SESSION?

» That those God calls, he empowers. God has promised by his Spirit that he will fuel the Church for all he has asked us to do.

» That the Church is the Community of the Spirit - not only the recipient of God's gifts and power, but the community within which he chooses to dwell.

» That the God who gives gifts in creation, and in the birth of each person, also give gifts at Pentecost, so that every person can live to the full and fulfill their promise and purpose.

» That the Holy Spirit journeys with us, forming in us the likeness of Christ. God will bring out the very best in each of us, and has purposes each one of us can serve.

» That the Spirit who is forming Christ in us is also forming the Church in the world, calling into being, in each new generation, the works of God.

We will discover that the Spirit is present with us, guaranteeing the fulfillment of every promise God has made and pointing us towards the future he has bought for us.

GIFTS AND GROWTH

Ken Robinson, who works with educators around the world to promote a greater degree of creativity in teaching, tells the story of an eight year-old girl who was failing badly in school. She was a fidget and struggled to concentrate. Her handwriting was poor. She would daydream in class or distract other students. Eventually she was taken to an educational psychologist, who spent timing talking to her and to her mother in his large oak-panelled office. Her school had referred her, suggesting that she had a learning disability and should perhaps be sent to a school for children with special needs. The eminent psychologist talked to the girl's mother, and to the girl herself, all the time observing her reactions. After a time he explained that he needed to speak privately to her mother out in the corridor, and that he would leave her alone in the office for a moment. Before leaving the room, he switched on a radio.

Outside the office, the psychologist asked the mother to wait for a moment, then to quietly observe, from a position out of sight, what her daughter was doing. Within minutes of being left alone, she was on her feet, moving gracefully and purposefully to the music coming from the radio. The beauty of her movements was staggering.

'You know,' the psychologist said, 'Your daughter isn't sick. She's a dancer. Take her to dance school.'

Gillian Lynne CBE explains that her mother did exactly as she had been asked. 'I can't tell you how wonderful it was,' she says, 'I walked into this room, and it was full of people like me. People who couldn't sit still. People who had to move to think.' [51] This took place in the 1930s and Gillian Lynne, now in her late 80s, has become one of the world's most successful choreographers. [52] She has danced with the Sadler's Wells Ballet and the Royal Ballet, appeared in West End and Broadway productions and on film and television, and has worked with Andrew Lloyd Webber on some of the most spectacular musicals in history, including *Cats* and The *Phantom of the Opera.* [53]

Workout
The Dancer Within You?

As you read Gillian Lynne's story, what does it make you think of? Do you see yourself as someone who has been misunderstood, or whose gifts have gone unnoticed? Are others around you in that same situation? To what extent do you think this kind of experience only happens for creative / talented / artistic people, or are there ways it might apply for all of us? What role can the Church play in helping us each discover 'the dancer within'?

There is nothing explicitly Christian about Gillian Lynne's story, yet it moves us as a picture of one person discovering her gifts - and of others being willing to nurture her in them. From that one moment of discovery and encouragement, a lifetime of dance has unfolded. The *discovery, development* and *deployment* of gifts is vital aspect of human growth. For the New Testament, it is the very heart of our growth in God. Paul's letter to the Ephesians, as we have seen, portrays a church committed to equipping *all* its members for life and mission. Chapter 4 expressed how this can happen, suggesting that:

» the key to equipping lies in discerning the callings God has for each person, and the gifts he gives for their fulfillment.

» this whole process is the work of the third person of the Trinity, *the Holy Spirit.*

For Paul, the mission of influencing and shaping the world is not only a task *to which* God calls the Church: it is a task *for which* he fuels and empowers her. The 'shining' of God's people is not achieved by the efforts of the humans involved, but by the Holy Spirit living in them, working through them and overflowing them. The Church is a living temple, [54] the dwelling place of the God, the community in whom the Holy Spirit lives. [55] God does not only declare a desire to shine through us, he establishes a method by which this will be possible.

51] Cited in Ken Robinson with Lou Aronica, *The Element: How Finding Your Passion Changes Everything,* Viking, 2009
52] See http://www.gillianlynne.com
53] See http://en.wikipedia.org/wiki/Gillian_Lynne
54] 1 Corinthians 3:16; 2 Corinthians 6:16; Ephesians 2:21
55] Ephesians 2:21

The Church will be empowered from within by God's Spirit. [56] God will place 'mighty power' on the inside of the believing community so that we will be able to achieve more than even the human imagination can conceive of. [57] The indwelling, empowering presence of the Spirit is essential to the Church's mission.

Further, this same Spirit [58] will give gifts to the body of Christ - gifts to each and every member, [59] and gifts to the body overall to provide for each member's equipping.[60] The whole operation is to be Spirit-soaked, a God-empowered adventure in a gift-giving economy. Paul is just as enthusiastic as Ken Robinson for each person to discover and use their God-given gifts: but he is convinced that it is only by the presence and power of God's Spirit that they will truly do so.

THE COMMUNITY OF THE SPIRIT

Paul does two things to make sure that his Ephesian readers understand the centrality, to their missional callings, of the Spirit's gifts. The first is to associate the giving of gifts with the Ascension of Christ. [61] This is a deliberate reference to the Day of Pentecost, reflecting the understanding of the early Church that it is through the Ascension of Christ that the release of the Spirit is made possible. [62] The Ascension is followed by - and makes possible - the Day of Pentecost. By connecting gift-giving with the Ascension in this way, Paul is in effect saying 'I'm talking here about the coming of the Spirit at Pentecost'.

The second thing he does in exploring the image of Ascension, is to choose an unusual translation (or mis-translation) from the Old Testament. Psalm 68 is a 'Psalm of Enthronement' picturing a victorious king newly enthroned in the midst of the people he has conquered. To mark his victory, and their new-found subjection to him, his enemies bring him gifts by way of tribute. *Their gifts to him* celebrate his Lordship over them. Psalm 68:18 captures the scene:

When you ascended to the heights, you led a crowd of captives. You received gifts from the people, even from those who rebelled against you. [63]

But Paul's chosen translation alters just a few words, and in the process re-frames the whole scene. He quotes:

When he ascended to the heights, he led a crowd of captives and gave gifts to his people. [64]

Paul is applying an accepted Rabbinic technique, whereby every possible translation can be a legitimate translation, and is using it for specifically Christological ends. Where every king before him has marked enthronement by receiving gifts, Jesus marks his victory by giving them. Christ's reign will be characterised by gift-giving. The community he calls into being, lives in, and empowers by his Spirit, will be formed by the receiving of his gifts. Paul's deliberate choice of this translation establishes once and for all a core truth of the Christian community: the Church of Jesus Christ will be built, human by human, through the pouring out of the Spirit's gifts.

56] Ephesians 3:16
57] Ephesians 3:20
58] Ephesians 4:4
59] Ephesians 4:7
60] Ephesians 4:11-12
61] Ephesians 4:8-10
62] See John 14:25-26; John 16:7; Acts 1:1-8
63] Psalm 68:18, NLT
64] Ephesians 4:8, NLT

HUMAN DYNAMITE

As the community of the Spirit the Church is the landing-place for the Spirit's gifts, and its every member is included in the gift-list. Discovering, developing and deploying the gifts the Spirit gives is the essence of Christian life and growth. This explains the 'how' of equipping. God's people will shine God's light to every corner of the culture because the Church, as a community indwelt by the Spirit, will discover and deploy God's gifts. God's people will discover that:

Each of us is gifted

Different gifts are given to different people, each one finding the unique combination of gift and call that marks out their vocational path. The Spirit is the one who empowers the life of faith. He brings life to gifts already given in creation, and he adds to them new gifts. Our 'natural' talents and the 'super-natural' gifts we may receive as followers of Christ, all come from the same Holy Spirit: our creator and our comforter; our redeemer and empowerer. As the Holy Spirit guides and empowers the Church, the gifts he has already given in creation come to life. He is at work both within and outside the Church, but it is in the Church, in the direct experience of his power and presence, that his gifts come into focus. As Simon Ponsonby writes,

'The Greek word for power is *dunamis* - from which we have derived words like dynamite, dynamo and dynamic. Christians who are filled with the Holy Spirit will be explosive; they will make a noise and an impact. Their words, lives and presence will change things. It is the fullness of that power that Paul wants us to enter into.' [65]

Together as the Church we find our gifts and grow in them

The leadership gifts given directly *to* the body of the Church are given so that other, wider gifts are found and used *in* the body of the Church. As the Church we participate in equipping one another - the goal is that *all* will be equipped. There is a process at work whereby we discover, through engagement with the Holy Spirit, what it is that God has gifted us and called us to do, and

So What?
A Gift Economy

How does the idea of God as 'the gift-giver' change your view of the Church? What would happen if your Church life was organised entirely around 'discovering, developing and deploying' God's gifts?

65] Simon Ponsonby, *More: How you can have more of the Spirit when you already have everything in Christ*, David C Cook, 2004

how we will do it. In the light of where God has placed us and of what he asks of us as disciples, we come to understand what we should do, and are aware of what we lack, and therefore we seek to be equipped.

The Spirit identifies the unique callings of each person, brings to light their God-given identity, and gifts them with new capacities. The term used for this process is *spiritual formation:* the Spirit forming in us the likeness and character of Christ, the *formation of the human spirit ... by the divine Spirit.* [66]

God's plans are revealed as the Spirit's gifts are discovered

The Church comes into being around the evident activity of God's Spirit. Because the Spirit is at work in each person, the contours of God's mission become visible as gifts are discovered. The term 'emerging church' has different meanings for different people in recent years, but in terms of the Spirit's work, the Church is *always* an emerging church. It is by God's Spirit at work in human lives that the Church is called into being. Peter, in Acts 10, opens the church to a whole new chapter of ministry to the Gentile community in response to the evidence of the Spirit's presence in individual lives. [67]

We do not lead the Holy Spirit into mission - we follow his evident activity. Specifically, this allows for the renewal of God's work in each new generation: the mission of God revealed as a new generation's gifts are discerned. This is a particular challenge at the stage in history at which we currently stand. As Alan Hirsch and Lance Ford challenge us:

All factors point to signs that Christianity is in decline in the West. We must own the fact that the way we live out our faith is culpable, at least in large part. A domesticated, tamed version of Christianity that is mired in the same wants, desires, and traps of the watching world yields no appeal ... For most of us, this means we must simply begin to step out beyond our self-imposed barriers of safety and security and risk, joining the Holy Spirit in what God is doing in our neighbourhoods and cities. [68]

66] Dallas Willard, *Spiritual Formation as a Natural Part of Salvation*, Presented at the 2009 Wheaton Theology Conference.
67] Acts 10:47
68] Alan Hirsch in Alan Hirsch and Lance Ford, *Right Here Right Now: Everyday Mission for Everyday People*, Baker Books, 2011

Workout
Where is the Spirit Working?

Alan Hirsch and Lance Ford imply that the Holy Spirit is at work already in our communities and cities: our job is to see what he is doing and join in. Is this something you find easy to accept, or does it seem strange to you? If God is already at work by his Spirit outside the church, what signs would you look for to discern his activity?

Speaker's Corner
The Best and Worst of the Church
Patrick Regan

What do you love most about the Church?
I love it when the Church isn't a place to attend but a community to be a part of. I love it when it reflects generosity, compassion and kindness to those around it, and I love that it is one of the few places you can really spend time with people from all walks of life that you wouldn't otherwise connect with.

What do you struggle with most about the Church?
I struggle with the politics which can often become a part of Church.

Paul's picture of God as a gift-giver and of the church as the community of the Spirit presents us with a number of significant avenues to explore. Specifically, this picture requires that we understand:

» That the Holy Spirit is **God's Gift to the Church.** Before we even begin to explore the gifts that the Spirit gives, we must acknowledge the the Spirit is himself a gift to us. Before he gives us anything else, God gives us himself. In creation as in redemption; in Eden as at Pentecost, God is the giver of gifts.

» That the Holy Spirit is the key to our **Formation in Christ.** God does not randomly distribute gifts without any sense of direction or purpose. Rather, he is shaping and moulding each one of us to reflect the character of Christ. We are being formed after the likeness of Christ: formation is the key process in which we experience the life of the Spirit.

» That the Holy Spirit renews the work of God in each **New Generation.** The Holy Spirit is not only forming each of us after the likeness of Christ, but is forming us together, as the Church, to fulfill God's purposes in our time and context. He is the deposit guaranteeing our inheritance, pointing us towards the plans of God. In each new generation, the voice of the Spirit calls the Church onwards to God's future.

GOD'S GIFT TO THE CHURCH

BEFORE HE IS THE BRINGER OF GOD'S GIFTS, THE HOLY SPIRIT IS HIMSELF GOD'S GIFT TO US

'Song of Songs 1:2 says, 'Let him kiss me with the kisses of his mouth' (NIV). The great twelfth-century Christian mystic Bernard of Clairvaux, reflecting on this verse, said, 'The Kiss of God is the gift of the Holy Spirit.' Bernard understood the Holy Spirit in terms of the kiss of love between the Father and the Son. This Holy Spirit given to us by Christ is God's kiss of love to us. By that same Spirit, in a cyclic movement, we kiss God in response.' [69]

Before we can even begin to explore the gifts *of* the Holy Spirit, we must stop to acknowledge the Holy Spirit *as* gift. Jesus describes the Spirit as a gift of the Father [70] and throughout the New Testament this is acknowledged. Before God even thinks of using us, he thinks of loving us. Any sense of participation in God's mission in the world begins with and is founded on our participation in his love. The Holy Spirit is not an impersonal force or influence: he is God's gift *of himself* to the church. As A W Tozer writes:

'Spell this out in capital letters: THE HOLY SPIRIT IS A PERSON. He is not enthusiasm. He is not courage. He is not energy. He is not the personification of all good qualities, like Jack Frost is the personification of cold weather. Actually, the Holy Spirit is not the personification of anything ... He has individuality. He is one being and not another. He has will and intelligence. He has hearing. He has knowledge and sympathy and ability to love and see and think. He can hear, speak, desire, grieve and rejoice. He is a person.' [71]

The third person of the divine Trinity, the Spirit is a gift freely given to the people of God. His presence cannot be bought or earned but flows from the generosity of God. The term *charismatic,* used to describe the presence and ministry of the Holy Spirit, is derived from the Greek *charis,* meaning 'favour' or 'grace'. Everything about the Spirit is *gift.*

Paul says, however, 'He who did not spare his own Son, but gave himself up for us, will he not freely give us all things?'. If you feel that you are not worthy to receive 'more' then you are right. You are not. But gifts are not based on the merit of the recipient, but on the generosity of the giver. God's heart is one of love for you. And he has more to give you. [72]

ROMANS 8:32

69] Simon Ponsonby, *More: How you can have more of the Spirit when you already have everything in Christ,* David C Cook, 2004
70] Matthew 7:11; Luke 11:13; Acts 1:4
71] A W Tozer, *The Counsellor: Straight Talk About the Holy Spirit from a 20th Century Prophet,* Christian Publications, 1993, cited in Robin Parry, *Worshipping Trinity: coming Back to the Heart of Worship,* Paternoster, 2005
72] Simon Ponsonby, *More: How You Can Have More of the Spirit When You Already Have Everything in Christ,* David C Cook, 2004

So What?
The Holy Spirit's Job Description

This session's study may well challenge your understanding of the Holy Spirit's work. One way to explore this is think through the job description the Holy Spirit has in the life of your Church. Start by reflecting on the way things are in your Church and write a paragraph that begins with the sentence:

'The things we expect the Holy Spirit to do in our Church are...' Be honest!

Then take some time to explore key New Testament passages about the Holy Spirit, some of which are touched on in this Theme Guide. Other examples are:
John 14:15-29, John 16:5-15, Acts 1:6-9, Acts 11:1-18, Acts 13:1-3, Romans 5:1-5, Romans 8:1-17 and 26-30, 2 Corinthians 1:21-22, Galatians 5:16-26, Hebrew 2:1-4, 1 John 2:26-27

(Find more passages by taking 'Holy Spirit' as a search term in the New Testament at www.biblegateway.com).

Write a second paragraph headed:
'The things the New Testament suggests that the Holy Spirit will do in our church are...'

What are the differences between the two paragraphs? How can this gap in expectations become fuel for your prayers for your church?

NO SPIRIT - NO CHURCH

In this sense there is no church that is not 'charismatic' - the church comes into being through the God's giving of himself in the Spirit. For missiologist Lesslie Newbigin, this is foundational to the very nature of the Church. Pentecost makes the Church possible.

'On that day [of Pentecost] we may say that everything was ready for the Church's life to begin. Christ's atoning work had been completed. His revelation of the Father in word and deed was compete. The nucleus of his Church was chosen and ready ... And yet, they had to wait. All was complete: and yet nothing was complete until the Spirit of God himself should be breathed into the new race of men. Only then, empowered by him, could they go forth to proclaim the message of salvation, and to baptise men in the name of Christ unto remission of their sins. In very truth it is the presence of the Holy Spirit that constitutes the Church.' [73]

Scot McKnight says of the Church of Acts:
'Something transforming and transcending happens immediately when you cross the threshold from the Gospels into that fifth book. Jesus' followers become the Church community that acts like kingdom community. Why? The Spirit of God is present. The Gospels lead to the Acts, because the kingdom dream of Jesus forms Spirit-transforming communities.' [74]

73] Lesslie Newbigin, *The Household of God*, SCM, 1953; Paternoster, 1998
74] Scot McKnight, *One Life: Jesus Calls, We Follow*, Zondervan, 2010

Workout
Location, Location, Location

Consider the following descriptions of homes or 'dwelling places'. For most of us, a dwelling place is a house. For a king, a dwelling place is a palace. For a bird, a dwelling place is a nest. For a tiger, a dwelling place might be the jungle. For a hermit crab a dwelling place is an unused sea-shell...
Now think of Paul's description of the Church as the dwelling place of the Spirit. What does it mean for the Holy Spirit to be 'at home' among God's people. What challenges does such an image present us with?

GIVER OF GIFTS

Whilst the outpouring of the Holy Spirit at Pentecost is a new event in the history of God's people, the association of the Spirit with 'gifts' and 'gifting' has deep Old Testament roots. The intimacy with God that becomes possible in the New Testament as a daily reality is foreseen in earlier generations in fragmented but significant episodes. One of the earliest glimpses of this intimacy is given in the book of Exodus, when the artist Bezalel is described as 'filled with the Spirit of God', enabling him to co-operate with God's remarkable plans.

'Bezalel executes in miniature the divine creative role of Genesis 1 in the building of the tabernacle. The Spirit of God with which the craftsmen are filled, is a sign of the living, breathing force that lies behind the completing of the project just as it lies behind the creation. Their intricate craftsmanship mirrors God's own work.' [75]

In the great adventure of creating the tabernacle, Bezalel is given an assistant, Oholiab (Exodus 31:6) and whole teams of artists and craftsmen are recruited to work with them (Exodus 35:10). The people are given the opportunity to contribute gold and silver, fine linen and threads: all the beautiful and valuable resources with which the tabernacle will be made (Exodus 35:5). Significant artistic talents; finely-honed craftsmanship; quality materials; the gifts of many people – these are the ingredients of which worship is created in the wilderness. This is to be a place in which the best is given to God, a space of beauty and peace inspired by God's Spirit. [76] This remarkable picture anticipates the gift-receiving economy Paul sees for the whole Church. It is the first mention in scripture of individuals being filled with God's Spirit: the first link in a chain of the Spirit's activity leading up to the coming of Christ. Simon Ponsonby writes:

'Bezalel, we are told twice, was filled with God's Spirit and the ability and intelligence of all craftsmanship to work artistically in gold, silver, bronze and stone. This man was set apart by God to help design all the utensils and furnishings for God's holy tabernacle

75] Terence Fretheim, *Interpretation: Exodus*, John Knox, 1991
76] Gerard and Chrissie Kelly, *Intimate with the Ultimate*, Authentic, 2009

(Exodus 31:2ff; 35:30). Joshua was filled with the Spirit of God and empowered to lead the people of Israel into the Promised Land, defeating Israel's enemies and claiming their promised inheritance (Deuteronomy 34:9). John the Baptist was filled with the Holy Spirit from birth, set apart and anointed to be the forerunner of Christ, preparing the way for the King (Luke 1:15). His mother Elizabeth was filled with the Spirit when she encountered Mary pregnant with King Jesus, and she prophesied over our Lord's mother blessing, revelation and encouragement (Luke 1:41ff). Similarly, her husband Zechariah, John's father, was filled with the Holy Spirit and prophesied concerning his son and his part in the salvation history of God. What a glorious thing - each member of that family filled by the Spirit, each member receiving revelation and prophetic utterance.' [77]

'NATURAL' AND 'SUPERNATURAL'

These examples, exceptional in their own day, become normative for the New Testament Church; the Spirit given to each and to all. Bezalel's human talents are both attributed to and enlivened by the Holy Spirit. So the Holy Spirit anoints the giftings of each member of the Church, and adds new gifts where these are needed: so that each of us can contribute our silver threads to God's tapestry. Both 'natural' and 'supernatural' gifts are included, attributed to the same Holy Spirit. God's actions in creation [78] at every birth [79] and in every life[80] demonstrate that the Spirit who is poured out on the Church at Pentecost [81] is by no means visiting our planet for the first time! Wolfhart Pannenberg writes:

'The same Holy Spirit of God who is given to believers in a wholly specific way, namely, so as to dwell in them (Romans 5:9, 1 Corinthians 3:16), is none other than the Creator of all life in the whole range of natural occurrence and also in the new creation of the resurrection of the dead... The work of the Spirit of God in his Church and in believers serves the consummating of this work in the world of creation.' [82]

In this sense we would affirm that Ken Robinson, in telling the story of Gillian Lynne, *is* talking about the gifts of the Spirit. Though his role may not be acknowledged, the Holy Spirit is the one who, in creation and at our birth, gives the gifts of God to humanity. All talents are God-given. This is implicitly acknowledged even in our secular culture, where the only language we can find to describe the special capacities we see in each other is the biblical language of 'talent' and 'gifting'. *Britain's Got Talent* is a profoundly biblical statement.

Workout
Gifts, Strengths or Talents

The language of gifts we are using here deliberately includes the gifts we think of as 'natural' - gifts that come to us at our birth as part of our created nature - and the gifts we call 'supernatural' - those given directly by the Holy Spirit as an outworking of Pentecost. Does it make sense to you to see **both** *these as gifts of the same Spirit? How does the work of the Spirit in your life relate to these different categories of gift?*

77] Simon Ponsonby, *More: How You Can Have More of the Spirit When You Already Have Everything in Christ*, David C Cook, 2004
78] Genesis 12:2
79] Psalm 139:7-14
80] Acts 17:25-28
81] Acts 2:1-4
82] Wolfhart Pannenberg, cited in Veli-Matti Kärkkäinen, *An Introduction to Ecclesiology: Ecumenical, Historical and Global Perspectives*, IVP, 2002

A COMMUNITY OF GIVING

In the Spirit, the receiving community becomes a giving community. As Bezalel and Oholiab surrender their giftings to serve the wider community, and as the people provide the resources needed, so each of us is given gifts *to be used for the benefit of others and for the greater glory of God.* Christopher Webb writes:

'One of the most striking aspects of the way the Spirit gives gifts to God's people is that the spiritual gifts are always given in order to be given again. If the Holy Spirit wishes to give a gift of healing, he rarely gives it to the one suffering from illness or disability. The Spirit gives the gift of healing to another, so that other will have the opportunity to show love to the one who suffers. And so it is with almost every gift: God gives prophecy to one to share with all; he gives insight to this woman to help her counsel this man; he gives wisdom to a child to enrich an adult.' [83]

This sets the Church apart as a community of gift-giving and gift-sharing, where the generosity of the God who has gifts for all is reflected in the generous use to which those gifts are put. Kester Brewin suggests that this principle is essential to the witness of the Church today:

'All churches, wherever they are and whatever tradition, need to become places in their communities where people can exchange gifts - not just spiritual gifts but any gifts: providing toddler groups, creating places to hang art, opening cafes for passersby, providing peaceful refuges from noisy streets, running seminars, making available financial advice, and providing practise rooms for young bands. In the exchange of gifts, relationships are always catalyzed, always strengthened. Then and only then can the talk turn to the one who gave everything for us.' [84]

So What?
Gift Inventory

*There are a number of 'Gift Inventories' you can get hold of that help individuals to identify the gifts God has given them. Some are restricted to the New Testament lists of supernatural giftings, while others are wider. What about widening the whole exercise to include the body of your local **ekklesia,** as far as you are familiar with it?*

Reflect on those you know in your church and try to list everyone you see as 'gifted' in any way. Try to be as comprehensive as possible. What is their talent or capacity that leads you to say this? How did you become aware of their 'giftedness'? If others from your faith community are on this journey with you, share your list with them and ask them to share theirs. If a group of you are involved, pool your lists.

*Now ask yourselves, what would the life of your church look like if the Holy Spirit were invited to take-hold of, anoint and ignite **all** these gifts?*

83] Christopher S Webb, *Becoming Like Jesus: The Spirit Empowered Life*, Renovare, www.renovare.us
84] Kester Brewin, cited in Eddie Gibbs and Ryan K Bolger, *Emerging Churches: Creating Christian Community in Postmodern Cultures*, Baker Academic, 2005

GIFTS OF ENCOURAGEMENT

Central to this gift economy will be the capacity of the Christian community to encourage. Believing that every person is gifted; that every person has a contribution to make; that God has prepared, for every person, works to fulfill, we should surely be the world's most energetic encouragers, cheering one another on to the fulfillment of God's purposes. Perhaps more of us should more earnestly seek the *gift* of encouragement.[85] Ajith Fernando writes:

'People are exposed to a lot of discouragement and rejection from others... May we be people who remind others of their potential under God and help them 'fan into flame the gift of God. (2 Timothy 1:6)' [86]

So What?
Be a Barnabas

Paul's close friend Barnabas was known as a 'son of encouragement'. His reputation in the Church was such that others felt more confident in their gifting as a result of being with him. Where do you see such a gift at work in the Church today? Where do you see it more needed? What steps would you need to take for your church to become the kind of community Ajith Fernando describes?

Speaker's Corner
The Best and Worst of the Church
Andy Frost

What do you love most about the Church?
Being part of a community sharing in a vision and commitment to being transformed and bringing about transformation.

What do you struggle with most about the Church?
Church politics!

85] Romans 12:8
86] Ajith Fernando, *Jesus Driven Ministry,* Crossway Books, 2002

FORMATION IN CHRIST

THE SPIRIT WORKS PATIENTLY WITH US AND IN US, TO FORM IN US THE LIKENESS OF CHRIST

If Paul is clear that the Spirit has gifts for each and for all, and that the discovery and deployment of those gifts is central to the life of the Church, he is also clear that this is not an instant or an easy process. His emphasis is on maturity, measured not as 'the best we can get in the circumstances' but against the highest of possible standards - the very stature of Christ. [87] This is a long-term, continuous, life-wide process. The Holy Spirit will work and wrestle with each of us to bring us to maturity. The traditional term for this process is 'spiritual formation' - the formation *of* the human spirit *by* the Holy Spirit. Dallas Willard writes:

'Spiritual formation for the Christian basically refers to the Spirit-driven process of forming the inner world of the human self in such a way that it becomes like the inner being of Christ himself.' [88]

Spiritual formation makes a strong link between the gifts of the Holy Spirit and the spiritual disciplines of learning and giving in faith. Both involve relationship with the same Holy Spirit, who both gifts us and equips us. This is the 'how' of equipping. It is by formation that the people of God are equipped to make a difference in the banks and schools and factories that surround us. James C Wilhoit, in *Spiritual Formation As If The Church Mattered* lists several images offered in the Bible for this process of spiritual growth:

» **Potter and clay** (Isaiah 64:8) God shapes us according to his will

» **Apprentice / disciple** (Luke 6:40) Jesus teaches, we learn

» **Vine and branches** (John 15:5) As we hold to Christ, we grow to bear fruit

» **Hunger and thirst** (Matthew 5:6) Those who seek God earnestly will find him

» **Famine / drought** (Amos 8:11) God stimulates our hunger for his word

» **Growth** (1 Corinthians 3:6-7) Others may help, but it is God who causes growth

» **Human growth** (1 Peter 2:2-3) Like infants we grow by the milk of God's word

» **Plants (Jeremiah** 17:7-8) We flourish and bear fruit when we trust in God

» **Heart and soul** (Proverbs 4:23) We guard our hearts as the spring of life [89]

Wilhoit also highlights the different actions associated in scripture with discipleship and growth:

» **Journeying** (3 John 6-7)

» **Coming home** (Zephaniah 3:20)

» **Brokenness** (Psalm 137:3)

» **Athletics** (1 Corinthians 9:25)

» **Putting on and taking off clothes** (Romans 13:12, Colossians 3:12)

» **Battle and struggle** (Ephesians 6:11-12)

» **Running the race** (Hebrews 12:1) [90]

Several factors are common to these images and actions, threaded as they are through the Old and New Testaments. They each allude to the passing of time; to the importance of work, effort and investment; to the twin goals of growth and fruitfulness and to God's dynamic participation in the process. Spiritual formation is *gospel-driven, Spirit-empowered, disciplined change*, built on *trust in God.*

87] Ephesians 4:13
88] Dallas Willard, *Renovation of the Heart: Putting on the Character of Christ*, Navpress, 2002
89] James C Wilhoit, *Spiritual Formation As If the Church Mattered: Growing in Christ Through Community*, Baker Academic, 2008
90] James C Wilhoit, *Spiritual Formation As If the Church Mattered: Growing in Christ Through Community*, Baker Academic, 2008

Workout
Pathways to Growth

Which of the 12 metaphors of growth and change given above is most descriptive of God work in your life? Which is the least familiar to you? If you were to choose one as a pathway of growth for the coming season, what would it be? What steps do you think you could take to embrace this change?

GOSPEL-DRIVEN

Spiritual formation, then, is never an event: it is always a process. It involves, over time, the transformation of a human being through engagement with God. Spiritual formation is not self-improvement, it is gospel-driven change. Wilhoit writes:

The primary motivation behind formation involves understanding the gospel and seeing its fruit grow in our lives. Spiritual formation is a result of gospel ministry because the way a non-Christian becomes a Christian and the way we grow *as* Christians are actually the same - believing the gospel more and more. In our culture of self-improvement, which has turned spirituality into a narcissistic pursuit, it seems vital that we do not see spiritual formation as just another route to personal empowerment. Spiritual formation is first and foremost about the gospel. [91]

Spiritual formation is not solely a cognitive process - the gospel that transforms us does not address our minds alone, but calls us to love God with our 'heart, mind, soul and strength'. It is not about learning or repeating words, or assenting to propositions. It is, rather, about our whole being, in all its dimensions, conforming to the pattern of Christ. It is learning to love and serve in our actions *and* our thinking, about letting the character and wisdom of God shape everything we are. There has been a perhaps dangerous divergence in many of our churches, where 'receiving the gifts' and 'growing in the disciplines' have been seen as two very separate pursuits, even as mutually exclusive. But the New Testament offers no such choice. Both, it insists, are part of our discipleship and both are the work of the Holy Spirit. How might we aspire, in our own time and culture, to be 'deep in the disciplines *and* strong in the Spirit?

Workout
Stick to the Script

If spiritual formation is 'gospel-driven', as James Wilhoit suggests, then there will be a significant role in it for scripture - the primary means by which God's story is made known to us. What are the ways that you can engage with scripture as part of your spiritual formation? Which have you tried? Which do you find easy, and which hard? Are there steps you can take for your own journey to be more fully shaped by scripture?

91] James C Wilhoit, *Spiritual Formation As If the Church Mattered: Growing in Christ Through Community*, Baker Academic, 2008

SPIRIT-EMPOWERED

If the gospel is the source and guide to spiritual formation, its active agent is the Holy Spirit himself - the presence of God made real for each believer. It is by the Spirit's actions in us that we grow, and it is in discovering the Spirit's gifts that we find fulfillment and fruitfulness. The Spirit forms us after the likeness of Christ. Simon Ponsonby writes:

'The Spirit comes to make Jesus Lord in our lives (1 Corinthians 12:2). The Spirit comes to transform us into the likeness of Christ (2 Corinthians 3:18ff), removing the marks of the flesh... that fallen sinful nature (Galatians 5:16-21), and to conform us to the sweet divine character (Galatians 5:22ff). The Spirit comes to empower us for service and witness to Christ (Acts 1:8)... This Holy Spirit, this divine dynamite, is dangerous. He blows where he wills, he goes where he wills, he will take us where he wills, he will break us as he wills, he will make us as he wills, he will use us as he wills (John 3:8).' [92]

The presence and empowerment of the Spirit, then, are given to us so that we become more Christ-like. There is an end-goal in view, and all the Spirit's gifts and ministries move towards this end.

'The key work of the Holy Spirit in our lives is the forming of Christ-like character in us. Paul writes in 2 Corinthians 3:17-18: 'Now the Lord is the Spirit, and where the Spirit of the Lord is, there is freedom. And all of us, with unveiled faces, seeing the glory of the Lord as though reflected in a mirror, are being transformed into the same image from one degree of glory to another; for this comes from the Lord, the Spirit.' Paul seems intentionally to blur the distinction between Jesus and the Holy Spirit as he affirms the role the Spirit plays in transforming us, step by step, into the likeness of Christ.' [93]

CHRISTOPHER WEBB WRITES

DISCIPLINED

Our part in this process is to develop the disciplines and practices that make us ready to receive God's Spirit, and to co-operate with his work in our lives. It is God who does the work in us, but our work is to let him do it! As Richard Foster writes:

Frankly, no Spiritual Disciplines, no Spiritual Formation. The Disciplines are the God-ordained means by which each of us is enabled to bring the little, individualised power pack we all possess—we call it the human body—and place it before God as 'a living sacrifice' (Romans 12:1). It is the way we go about training in the spiritual life. By means of this process we become, through time and experience, the kind of person who lives naturally and freely in 'love, joy, peace, patience, kindness, generosity, faithfulness, gentleness, and self-control' (Galatians 5:22-23). [94]

Similarly, Dallas Willard insists that while our salvation is entirely the work of grace, there is nonetheless work to be done in us. Our growth in the spiritual disciplines enables us to receive and process more of God's grace in our lives: to extend the reach of grace ever more deeply into our hearts and characters.

'As an apprentice of Christ, I may be saved by grace, but I still have years of habitual anger, materialism, lust, and many other things to be dealt with. They're not just going to go away. Like someone who has a bad golf swing and always slices off to the right, I'm going to have to practise hitting the ball in a different way to make it go straight. The slice is in my body; it's how I have been formed. The disciplines help transform my habitual actions. The disciplines are not a substitute for grace, but receptacles for it.' [95]

Transformation by the power of the Spirit is not a spectacular, otherworldly process. It is embedded in life's realities; worked out in the highs and lows of our everyday world.

'Christian spiritual formation is really hammered out in the harsh realities of ordinary life - ear infections and broken arms and bosses filled with guile and stock market slumps and neighbours who deceive. Hence, these are the very places where our hardest study and most careful work in spiritual formation must go on.' [96]

92] Simon Ponsonby, *More: How You Can Have More Of The Spirit When You Already Have Everything In Christ,* David C Cook, 2004
93] Christopher S Webb, *Becoming Like Jesus: The Spirit Empowered Life, Renovare,* www.renovare.us
94] Richard Foster, Renovare Newsletter May 2003 http://www.renovare.us/ViewNewsLetter/tabid/2404/Default.aspx?ID=71
95] Dallas Willard, interview at http://www.dwillard.org/articles/artview.asp?artID=112
96] Richard Foster, Renovare Newsletter May 2003 http://www.renovare.us/ViewNewsLetter/tabid/2404/Default.aspx?ID=71

So What?
Deep in the Disciplines

In **Celebration of Discipline** Richard Foster lists twelve distinct spiritual disciplines, categorising them as Inward, Outward and Corporate in nature. He lists:

» The inward disciplines of Meditation, Prayer, Fasting and Study

» The outward disciplines of Simplicity, Solitude, Submission and Service

» The corporate disciplines of Confession, Worship, Guidance and Celebration [97]

There are other lists of disciplines, and more could be added to this one, but Foster suggests that these twelve represent the major ways by which the followers of Christ, down through history, have been able to engage with God's transforming presence in their lives. In looking at the list, how many of these disciplines are familiar to you as an aspect of your experience of God? How many are completely unknown to you? Are there steps you can take to explore disciplines you have not known to date? In the setting of the local church, how are these disciplines resourced and encouraged? What would a church look like if it's structures and programmes were designed to offer all its members help and support in these areas?

BUILT ON TRUST

At the heart of formation is the need for trust. We trust ourselves to the ministry of God's Spirit within us. We trust ourselves to the process, and to the assurance that God desires the very best for us. We welcome the work of the Spirit in our lives because we trust the goals he has for us. Carolyn Ros, writing of the trial of walking with her husband through a catastrophic illness, says:

Hope is anchored in who God is and the promises that he has made. When we put our trust in him, he has promised never to leave us or forsake us. Whatever takes place in our lives, he does have a bigger picture. He desires to show us how it all fits into his eternal design for us. Life is so much more than just the few years that we live here on earth. Live this life in view of eternity. [98]

BETTER TOGETHER

Crucial to the understanding of spiritual formation is the corporate nature of God's work in us. There are aspects of formation that are worked out by the individual, and there are times when solitude is essential to the process. No-one else can take responsibility for the challenges God places on me - but there is a wider sense in which all formation is corporate. It is through the Church that the Holy Spirit reaches us. In community; in submission to one another; in the hard work of being and building family, I discover paths of personal growth. To perceive of spiritual formation as the responsibility of the isolated individual is to miss a whole dimension of its impact. God calls us to journey together; to love and support one another. There are challenges to being community, but there are also joys, and it is in community that God forms us. It is in this dimension that the biblical view of formation most challenges the contemporary search for an individualised self-fulfillment available to consumers at their convenience. The involvement, in formation, of spiritual directors is a step away from individualism, but the Bible calls for more than even this: it calls us to be formed in community.

97] Richard Foster, *Celebration of Discipline*, Hodder and Stoughton, 1984
98] Carolyn Ros, *Broken Dreams, Fulfilled Promises*, Kingsway, 2006

Workout

Honesty Required

The paragraph above suggests that spiritual formation functions best in community: the church is our key to being spiritually formed. But many people, in honesty, find the reverse to be true. Church activities demand so much of their time and the church vision calls so much for their attention, that the priority of their own growth and development gets lost. Far from resourcing formation, church seems to get in its way. Some believers take the only road open to them in response: to embrace spiritual formation as a personal, private and solitary pursuit. Too many grow in Christ in spite of the Church rather than because of it. Is this your experience or that of others you know? If it is, what do you think the answer is? Is it possible for the corporate benefits of formation to be let loose in our churches? Consider the two-fold challenge:

1. What gets in the way of our church being a vital centre of spiritual formation?

2. What can we do to put this right?

You might want to reflect, in this, on the vital role that small groups have played for many in the journey of spiritual formation. From Wesley's 'class meetings' through to contemporary cell groups and even Alpha Courses, believers have often found the setting of a small group to be an aid to their formation. Has this been your experience?

Take a moment to pray for your church group or congregation, and for the wider body of Christ. Pray that we will find the motivation and the resources we need to become a genuine source of formation.

WAVES OF CHANGE

Viv Thomas is founder and director of 'Formation', an organisation that works across Church denominations to develop resources for personal growth and change, using a central model of spiritual formation. He reflects here on six waves of change that are currently impacting the Church in its response to spiritual formation.

Six Waves

In Formation our desire is to assist the Church and her leaders in developing 'spectacular ordinary lives'. We see a series of waves hitting the Church in the United Kingdom as we try to do this. Here are some of the bigger waves that come in no particular order of priority.

Wave One: We are seeing an increase in cleverness and decrease in wisdom. On one side the Church is cleverer than she has ever been, but she may be less discerning than at any previous time in history. We have more information than ever, but seem to be forgetting how to live wisely and well.

Wave Two: There is an increased desire for the 'quick fix' and decreased desire for the slow rhythmic walk with Jesus through the spiritual disciplines. We can be pumped up in a brief spiritual sprint, but settling in for the marathon of social and spiritual heavy lifting in one location is another thing. There are exceptions to this but this wave is on the rise. God does some of his work very quickly, but each breakthrough has to be incorporated into the slow walk.

Wave Three: There is an increase in distraction and decrease in attentiveness. Flickering screens, 24-hour rolling news and a twitching culture is having its effect on our individual and communal ability to focus on what we should be doing and doing it.

Wave Four: There is a decreased emphasis on formality and an increased focus on relationships. This has been going on for a while and looks set to continue because more and more of us live our lives alone. One of the effects of this is that people are mentor-hungry. Interestingly, in the middle of this wave is an increasing desire for the structure of Spirit-filled or Spirit-inspired liturgy.

Wave Five: There is a decrease in judgementalism and an increase in tolerance. People are able to hear some new emphasis or teaching, process it and then absorb it into their particular scheme for living. We seem more than happy to learn from other trends, movements or ecclesial tribes around the globe, filleting out what we consider to be good and discarding the rest. People have a wide vision of what constitutes the Church.

Wave Six: There is a decreased emphasis on doctrine and an increased emphasis on feeling. We don't know the Bible very well but our therapists of various kinds are busy. Wonderfully, people are more able to acknowledge their emotions but ignorance of scripture always causes problems. People have an insufficient story in their hearts, no place where they can hang their emotions and pray for them appropriately.

All of these waves meet, merge and cause other waves and ripples to be created. What are the underlying conditions which seem to be creating these waves? The two contradictory forces of fear and love are surging below the surface. Some in the Church are fearful and therefore both paralysed and caged, eventually collapsing into consumerism or something similar as an alternative to facing real life. But, there are many more experiencing an unprecedented outpouring of God's love showing itself in generosity, patience, courage and outrageous hope. How should we address these conditions? We need to develop the habits that help us pay attention to God. Our habits and imagination are closely linked. What we practise and imagine, we will become. Practice does not make perfect it makes permanent. We need to practise love for God, the Church and the world in the middle of self-forgetfulness. Our homes and work places are the primary places where these habits and practices need to be textured into our lives. Now what could those habits actually be?

Viv Thomas, Director of Formation and Honorary Teaching Pastor
at St Paul's Hammersmith www.formation.org.uk

So What?
Six Waves

*Read through Viv Thomas's 'Six Waves' of change, left. Which of these do you see evidence for in your own church and community? For each that you recognise, consider the SWOT implications - in what sense is this change a **Strength** to your church; in what sense is it a **Weakness**? What does it offer in terms of **Opportunity**, and what does it bring in terms of **Threat?***

How might your practice of the Christian life reflect what you have learned from this exercise?

A NEW GENERATION

THE SPIRIT RENEWS, IN EVERY GENERATION, THE WORK OF GOD IN THE WORLD

Psalm 78 gives a window into one of the strongest commitments of Hebrew culture - the commitment to pass faith on to each new generation. The Psalm explores the story of God in the context of faith transmission, declaring that:

We will tell the next generation the praiseworthy deeds of the LORD, his power, and the wonders he has done. [99]

and that

They would not be like their ancestors - a stubborn and rebellious generation [100]

Whilst this may be uncomfortable news for those described as a 'stubborn and rebellious generation' it is the best possible news for the Church. No matter how bleak our recent past has been, our future is not dictated by it. The giving of the Spirit makes possible the renewal of God's story in each new generation. God's Church is called into being anew by the actions of the Holy Spirit in every age. A new generation can at the same time be both *consistent with* the story of God and *different from their parents'* generation. The Spirit calls forth a Church that is shaped by past stories but not imprisoned by past mistakes. We look back, but we move forward. As New Zealand church-planter Steve Taylor writes:

'The Maori people of New Zealand have a phrase, *i nga ra o mua*. It means 'to walk forward, looking back'. The phrase urges walking into the future aware of one's roots and history...' [101]

SPIRIT OF RENEWAL

The 'shining' of God's wisdom into the world through the Church, and the work of the Holy Spirit to form Christ in each believer, are both concrete, historical processes. This is not a virtual or theoretical community of faith but a real movement, made up of real people in real social and political settings. Church is formed by the Spirit in specific contexts and will change as those contexts change. Part of what the Holy Spirit is doing in each generation is bringing to birth the newness God desires for his Church. As Hans Küng, one of the leading Catholic thinkers of our times has written: the Church...

'...must always be prepared to orientate itself anew, to renew itself. It must always be prepared to seek a new path.' [102]

This 'new path' will be discerned by watching for the actions of the Spirit in two distinct directions. Firstly, in the 'newness' of the rising generations within the Church itself and secondly, in the 'newness' of the cultural contexts in which they are called to bear witness to Christ. This means for the Western Church that our understanding of the Church itself, and of our responsibility to equip and release God's missional people, must take account of the changes in our technological, social, philosophical and global context. The generations in whom the Spirit is now at work are postmodern generations, and the cultures to which they are called are postmodern cultures.

I nga ra o

99] Psalm 78:4
100] Psalm 78:8
101] Steve Taylor, *The Out Of Bounds Church: Learning To Create A Community Of Faith In A Culture Of Change*, Youth Specialities, 2005
102] Hans Küng, *The Church*, Continuum, 2001

Workout
Spirit of Renewal

The assumption here is that one of the ways by which the Holy Spirit renews the work of God is to engage with, and reach out to, a new generation. In a transitional era, where a Church forged in the years of modernity must offer new hope to the generations of postmodernity, this will mean the Holy Spirit calling the Church to new ways of being. TTWWADI (That's the way we've always done it) won't wash. Do you have recent experience of the Holy Spirit calling your Church to new things? What were the circumstances and how did you respond? Share your experience with someone you don't know, and ask them to share with you their experience of following the Holy Spirit's voice.

Workout
Challenging Churches

How do you feel as you read these comments? Do you strongly agree with the sentiments expressed, or strongly disagree? Or are you able to accept them as someone else's view even though you do not share it? Imagine each of the above being shared with you by a friend, neighbour or colleague. How might you respond? What steps might you take, in each case, to address these concerns? What challenges do these views present to the churches of the UK?

UNCOMFORTABLE QUESTIONS

Many practising missioners hear the voice of the Spirit in the penetrating and, at times, uncomfortable questions being asked of the Church by new generations. Young people within the Church, young people who have walked away from the Church and young people who stand, as observers, outside the Church, may all have things to say to us through which we might hear God speak. In the US context Dan Kimball has interviewed a significant number of young leaders in postmodern settings to discover their views of Church. The resulting book *They Like Jesus But Not The Church*, is very much an American project, but has lessons nonetheless that resonate with the European scene. The six areas in which Kimball found disparities between the way churches view themselves and the way young adults view them are summarised as:

» The Church is an organised religion with a political agenda
» The Church is judgemental and negative
» The Church is dominated by males and oppresses females
» The Church is homophobic
» The Church arrogantly claims all other religions are wrong
» The Church is full of fundamentalists who take the whole Bible literally [103]

So What?
He Who Has Ears...

The crucial aspect of Kimball's work is not to ask whether you agree or not with these claims, it is to understand that they are the claims that many people make. Kimball and others are asking us to hear what the Holy Spirit might be saying to us in the words of a rising generation. Is this a conversation you, too, have heard?

103] Dan Kimball, *They Like Jesus But Not The Church: Insights Irom Emerging Generations*, Zondervan, 2007

Of particular importance is the fact that these views are not limited to young adults   the Church. Very often, they are expressed within our faith communities. Describing the growth of 'alternative worship' communities in the UK, Andy Thornton, co-founder of the innovative 'Late Late Service' in Glasgow and a former director of the Greenbelt Festival, asserts that:

'It is not only missional questions that drive the impetus for creating new forms of Church. What plays a major role in new forms of Church is simply the desire for lifelong Christians to make sense of their two worlds: their Church and their culture. The people who care most about the cultural disconnect within the Church are the kids of the people in Church ... These kids want to stop being cultural outsiders. They look to bring their two worlds together. They seek authenticity and, in so doing, they need to end the dissonance.' [104]

This is an important insight because it tells us that it is not only our missional context that has changed in the shift to a postmodern worldview, but that those we need to equip for mission in this context are themselves shaped by it. 'Postmodernism' used to describe a specific philosophical movement that questioned many of the assumptions of the modern era: but it has come to mean much more. The movement itself came to have such an influence on education and the media, that it is fair to use the term now to describe the context of a whole generation. Postmodernity is the setting in which we now find ourselves, and it is crucial that the Church makes a response.

Consider these further comments from Dan Kimball's US interviewees. Can we hear the renewing voice of the Spirit in these questions?

'I call the Church 'organised religion' because if I am praying on my own, when ever I want, there is such freedom in that. But then I go to a church and some one is there to say, 'Stand up now,' 'Sit down now,' 'Sing this now,' 'Listen to me now,' 'Do what I say now'' 'Act like this now.' It's kind of like a religious Simon Says. Why go through all that when it can be much more natural praying and talking to the Good Lord on my own without all that extra control?' [105]

'I did grow up in a church, but now I am a Buddhist. When I became a mother, I wanted my daughter to have a spiritual upbringing. However, I didn't want her to become like the Christians in the church I knew. They were always so negative and complaining about everything, and I wanted my daughter to be in a positive environment. I became a Buddhist since they are much more loving and peaceful people than those in the Church.' [106]

'I would be totally into going to a church if the church revolved more around the person of Jesus than around the personality of the pastor. I'd be totally interested in going if the church were more about helping and loving other people than about criticising and condemning other people.' [107]

There is an inherent negativity in these comments that is perhaps hard to read. Those of us who love the Church, and celebrate its strengths every day, struggle to accept these observations. But they are honest accounts of real lives, and they do represent the experience of many. Holding such observations in tension with all we know to be positive and beautiful about God's Church, what can we learn from listening to such voices?

LOVING THE CHURCH

Dan Kimball's phrase 'They like Jesus but not the Church' has come to symbolise one of the greatest challenges to mission in the new generation. Both Henri Nouwen and, more recently, Tim Keller, have warned of the danger of this situation. Henri Nouwen writes:

'When we say 'I love Jesus, but I hate the Church,' we end up losing not only the Church but Jesus too. The challenge is to forgive the Church. This challenge is especially great because the Church seldom asks us for forgiveness.' [108]

Keller insists, on a very practical basis, that the link between faith and community - between finding Christ and finding a place in his Church - cannot be broken:

104] Andy Thornton, cited in Eddie Gibbs and Ryan K Bolger, *Emerging Churches: Creating Christian Community in Postmodern Cultures*, Baker Academic, 2005
105] Gary', cited in Dan Kimball, *They Like Jesus But Not The Church: Insights From Emerging Generations*, Zondervan 2007
106] 'Jennnine', cited in Dan Kimball, *They Like Jesus But Not The Church: Insights From Emerging Generations*, Zondervan 2007
107] 'Gary', cited in Dan Kimball, *They Like Jesus But Not The Church: Insights From Emerging Generations*, Zondervan 2007
108] Henri Nouwen, *Bread for the Journey*, cited in Dan Kimball, *They Like Jesus But Not The Church: Insights From Emerging Generations*, Zondervan 2007

'I realise that so many people's main problem with Christianity has far more to do with the Church than with Jesus. They don't want to be told that to become a Christian and live a Christian life they need to find a church they can thrive in. They've had too many bad experiences with churches. I fully understand. I will grant that, on the whole, churchgoers may be weaker psychologically and morally than non-churchgoers. That should be no more surprising than the fact that people sitting in a doctor's office are on the whole sicker than those who are not there. Churches rightly draw a higher proportion of needy people. They also have a great number of people whose lives have been completely turned around and filled by the joy of Christ ... I realise how risky it is to tell my readers that they should seek out a church. I don't do it lightly, and I urge them to do so with the utmost care. But there is no alternative. You can't live the Christian life without a band of Christian friends, without a family of believers in which to find a place.' [109]

Workout
Challenging Churches

How do you feel on reading Keller's statement that 'there is no alternative. You can't live the Christian life without a band of Christian friends, without a family of believers in which to find a place.' Can you support this claim, or would you encourage those carving out a solo faith to continue? If you agree with Keller, what would you say are the difficulties associated with 'going it alone'? What would you say to someone who is determined to be a follower of Jesus but equally determined not to be involved with the Church?

RE-IMAGINEERING THE CHURCH

If the assertion that 'Jesus without the Church' is not an option stands, then a significant challenge is presented to contemporary Western churches. The need to re-imagine ways of being Church that connect with and inspire the new generations becomes urgent. Can we recover a vision to inspire and equip a new generation? Where our models of Church are holding us back, will we allow the Holy Spirit to change them? Are we able to re-calibrate our churches as disciple-making communities for the postmodern generations? A good place to start is to examine *how* we do the things we do. The way we do things in our communities shape people just as much as what we say we want for them. The stories we tell, the heroes we honour, the way we welcome, the prayers we pray are all symptoms of who we are, and play a part in forming us for love and service.

Perhaps in this, the forming work we have already ascribed to the Holy Spirit in discovering, developing and deploying the gifts of God's people, is key. Might the key to *reaching* a new generation lie in the *anointing* of a new generation? Will we invite the Holy Spirit to gift our children in ways that go beyond their parents' experience? Might the answer to the challenges around us be found, after all, within our ranks? Keith Warrington, Dean of Studies at Regent's College in Malvern, offers a parable that might just point us in that direction. It is the story of a South African farmer

'...who sold his farm to search for diamonds. Unfortunately, although he travelled hundreds of miles, he never found any. In his despair he jumped into a river and drowned, a penniless failure whose dream had turned into desolation. A few years later, the man who had bought the farmer's land found an unusual rock and took it home, where it was noticed by a friend who later informed him that it was the biggest diamond that had ever been discovered. The farm was transformed into the Kimberly Diamond mine - the richest in the world.' [110]

109] Timothy Keller, *The Reason for God: Belief in an Age of Scepticism*, Hodder and Stoughton 2008
110] Dr Keith Warrington, Hope, Distance Learning Course by Regents Theological College

So What?
Find the Diamonds

Keith Warrington's diamond story implies that the answer to the problems we see outside the Church may lie within the Church. We may already have the gifts and resources we need to meet the challenges. Specifically, our young people may already have all that they need to engage with their own generation. If this is true, what can your church do to release these treasures?

This is a poem we have adopted as a prayer within the Bless Network, as we work and serve alongside a new generation. Is this a prayer you can pray in your local setting?

We believe every human being
has a worth worth seeing
Every name
Is a sound worth saying
Your potential
A prayer worth praying
You see coal - God sees diamonds

We believe in the grace
Of the gifts God gives
His breath
In everything that lives
Greater gifts to be discovered
Deep in you; disguised; dust-covered
You see coal - God sees diamonds

We see God seeking
A servant generation
Kindness as the kindling
To kick-start transformation
Love as liberation
of a captive creation
We are digging
for the diamonds God sees [111]

111] c. Gerard Kelly, April 2011, www.blessnet.eu

LOVE TRIANGLES

Matt Wilson

It's now 15 years since the first Eden team chose to become resident in one of Britain's most deprived council estates in order to be a catalyst for change. With a priority toward youth and a holistic vision for the whole community, Eden provides a great example of what can happen when evangelism and social justice are married together. There are now more than 20 Eden teams, serving communities up and down the country from Newcastle in the north to London in the south.

As you might expect there have been tremendous highs and lows over the years. Writing about Eden in his book *Citizens and Disciples* Bishop Graham Cray comments, 'The resulting work is seeing significant changes both in lives and in communities. It is not a quick fix, nor has it led to all the changes the teams would love to see, but it is evidence of the work of the Holy Spirit. In fact, the teams' capacity to stay and remain true to their vision long term is as much an evidence of the work of the Spirit as the changes and conversions which have taken place.' [112]

One important aspect of the vision that the teams have clung to over the years is the principle of remaining rooted in local church. There has been ample opportunity to 'go it alone' but this temptation has always been successfully resisted. You see, anyone who joins an Eden team is in that same action joining an Eden partner church, that's how we roll. Why? Because urban churches face an almost impossible missional task – reaching out to neighbourhoods which are home to the most jaundiced teenagers and the most dysfunctional families in the nation. For Eden, every hour spent with a young person, every residents' association meeting attended, every pound spent in the local shop, is an expression of the life of the partner church within the community it is committed to loving back to life.

Probably the highest privilege that an Eden team member has, is to serve their church in its mission of disciple-making. In the early years of Eden this was generally understood as the cultivation of a popular process known as 'belong, believe, behave'. However, over time Eden teams began to realise that it isn't a process at all. Rather, the 3 Bs form a triangle that reveals the true condition of a person's life. Let me explain…

Typically when we meet a young person on an estate they're living in a very small triangle – that is, they have very little sense of belonging to anything or anyone; they believe very little – in fact they tend to be consumed by suspicion and mistrust; and their behaviour is both self-destructive and causing pain to those around them. Eden's task is to lovingly, imaginatively and consistently offer opportunities to those we are drawn into relationship with – opportunities to grow their triangle! This is the work of disciple-making, and there are no short cuts to success. The investment of time is counted in years rather than weeks or months.

Is it worth it? Absolutely. Because as the years progress we see our teenagers growing in all three dimensions. They develop a strong sense of being part of a community that is bigger than they are – the Church, the family of God. They also grow a vibrant trust in a loving God who has a plan for their life and never gives up. And their behaviour, whilst still from time to time contradictory, is infinitely more healthy, a profound change evident for all to see.

Matt Wilson, National Director, Eden Network
www.eden-network.org

112] Graham Cray, *Disciples and Citizens: A Vision for Distinctive Living*, IVP, 2007

Speaker's Corner
The Best and Worst of the Church
Mark Greene

What do you love most about the Church?
The exhilaration of walking with such an extraordinary variety of grace-drenched people reflecting the glory and care of Jesus in a myriad ways.

What do you struggle with most about the Church?

So What?
Come Holy Spirit

If the Spirit is given to bring to life the potential of every human being who will receive him, and if the 'newness' of the Church in every generation is the Spirit's work, there is perhaps a prayer that we can always pray. No matter how desperate the situation of the Church may seem in our culture, three short words define our future: **Come Holy Spirit.** *Three words of invitation, addressed to the third person of the Trinity, might just change everything.*

Come Holy Spirit
In the places where we are dry and broken and have lost the joy of God...
Come Holy Spirit

*Where we face obstacles and challenges
that are too much for us.
Where our strength is simply not enough to get us through...*
Come Holy Spirit

*Where those we know and love are struggling.
Where friends and family need to know God's love;
to receive his grace; to be transformed by his power...*
Come Holy Spirit

*Where our cities struggle with the burden of too much sin;
too many questions;
too many false answers.
Where our nations flounder for the loss of their faith...*
Come Holy Spirit

*Come Holy Spirit to our families.
Come Holy Spirit to our neighbourhoods and towns.
Come Holy Spirit to our Church.*
To our homes and hearts: Come Holy Spirit. [113]

113] Gerard and Chrissie Kelly, *Intimate with the Ultimate*, Authentic, 2009

TAKE SPRING HARVEST HOME... TAKEAWAYS FROM HOPE

In this session we have seen the importance of gifts and character, and how God uses us through them. This is a truth brought to us powerfully through this session's notes but once again, why do we sometimes struggle so much to really believe that each one of us has gifts and a contribution and to allow our characters, our spiritual formation, to be changed?

Psychologists tell us that we have a script in our heads that speaks to us. Part of the tragedy of our Western culture is that, for lots of different reasons, so many are afflicted with a negative self image. Something in our past, in the voice of a teacher or a difficult experience, creates an inner script. Every time we hear something that tells us we have gifts and a contribution to make, that inner voice says 'not you, remember what happened last time, you are a failure, you can't make a difference'.

So part of this Takeaway is to recognise that we perhaps have something of this negative self image and to ask God to help us on this journey, and on this journey we need to believe afresh three things:

1. God is good; he is who he says he is.
2. We are who God says we are: his children born again by the Spirit of God, gifted and valued.
3. We can do what God says we can do.

But our Takeaway doesn't stop there. In the great commandment we are told not only to love God but to love our neighbour as ourselves. To love our neighbour means that we have a high view of people and we think people are significant and important. If we embrace this as a value, as part of our spiritual formation, and we take it with us into our world, whether in business, at home, or at school, college, or university, and when you treat the people who work, who sit beside you with respect, you care, you listen, you care for their spiritual and physical welfare in whatever way that you can, you bring a little bit of heaven into that space. A well known business man was challenged in this way and he realised that as he walked from the lift to his office he had walked past admin staff and helpers as if they did not exist, and he felt ashamed that he had not given them value. So one day he stopped by a lady he had walked past thousands of times and asked for her name. Day by day he started to show value in whatever way he could to the five or six desks he walked by. Slowly but surely a little bit of heaven arrived between lift and office door.

So the second part of the Takeaway is to change not only our self-image but our image of others. Can we treat others as loved, gifted and valued by God?

Laurence Singlehurst and Roy Crowne, HOPE, www.hopetogether.org.uk

Fresh Expressions: www.freshexpressions.org.uk

CELEBRATE GOD'S BRILLIANT IDEA

This session of the *Theme Guide* has asked us to explore the work of the Holy Spirit in the Church: his giving of gifts; his forming of us to be to be like Christ; his renewing of the works of God in each new generation. We have asserted the brilliance of God's idea to put the power for change *inside* each believer. What can we celebrate about this brilliant idea?

1. We can celebrate the fact that God does not call us to any task for which he is not willing to empower us. It is with his resources, not our own, that we launch out into his world.

2. We can rejoice in the sheer exuberance of receiving and knowing the Holy Spirit - the very person of God coming to live in us and with us.

3. We can love this community that is more than a mere collection of people but is the very dwelling place of God. We can thank God with all our hearts that he has made such a community possible.

4. We can be thrilled to see the many gifts God has given and is giving to our brothers and sisters in the Church, and to know that he will keep polishing each of them until they shine like diamonds. We can rejoice that every person we meet has the potential to shine in God's kingdom.

5. Perhaps more than anything, we can celebrate the remarkable truth that God chooses to live in us and with us: that he is fulfilling before our eyes the promise made to a prophet of long, long ago:

'**When this happens, O my people, you will know that I am the Lord. I will put my Spirit in you, and you will live again and return home to your own land. Then you will know that I, the Lord, have spoken, and I have done what I said. Yes, the Lord has spoken!**'[114]

114] Ezekiel 37:13, NLT

'3
help
them
love

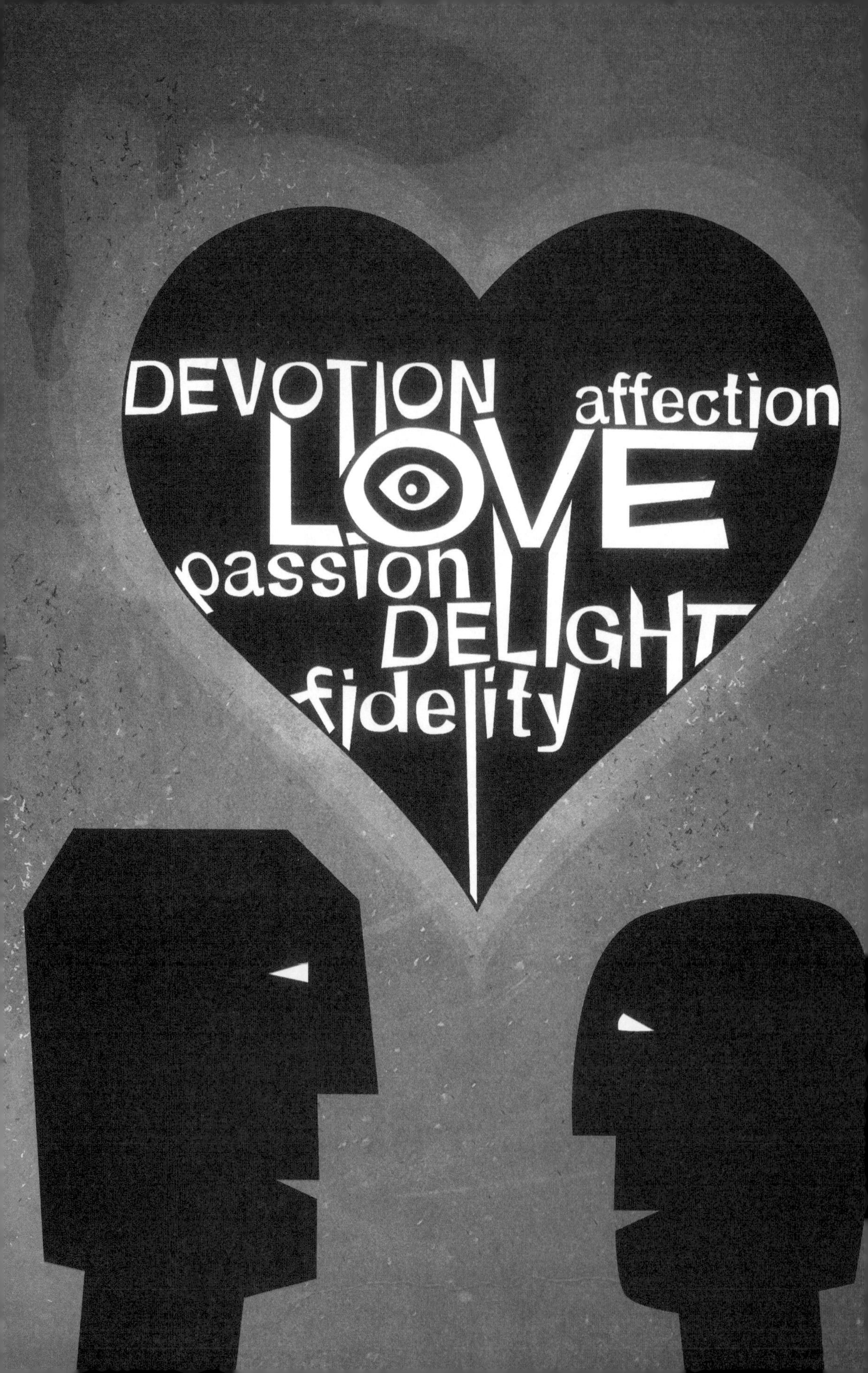
DEVOTION
affection
LOVE
passion
DELIGHT
fidelity

help them love

THE CHURCH AS THE BODY OF CHRIST

The call to the Church is to be like Jesus; to imitate and emulate his life and ministry. And if there is one word that sums up that life, it is love. Jesus loved in service; loved in teaching and caring; loved in healing and direction and encouragement and joy. His every action was qualified by love. And he calls us to follow this same path.

To accept God's invitation in Christ is to join a revolution of love. It is to be bring personal, relational, social and global transformation through self-giving love. When I become part of God's family, I discover that I am loved: the foundation of my life is the fact that God loves me. But, miraculously, I also discover a capacity to love others. This may begin with those near to me, but if I let it, it will soon spill over. I will find myself loving those I once thought unlovable, and doing for them the things that love demands that I should do.

Servanthood, to the follower of Christ, is not duty or drudgery. It is the overflow of God's love. It is joy and celebration: as much an act of worship as any song you will ever sing. The Church is called to be a servant community, living out the love of Christ, and through it discovering his joy.

WHAT WILL WE DISCOVER IN THIS *CHURCH ACTUALLY* SESSION?

» That the Church is the Body of Christ, called to continue his ministry and love in the world.

» That we are called to servanthood, turning the love of God into embodied acts of kindness.

» That God is honoured when the Church lives out the call to love.

» That God has a special place in his purposes for the poor - those who are most impacted by the absence of God's peace from the world. In the restoration of *shalom* that the kingdom will bring, the poor will be the first to see the difference.

» That through acts of love God is working to transform the world - acting through his people to extend love and grace from personal experience to social and global change.

» That God's mission in the world, by definition, includes both word and deed; both justice and justification; both the challenge to personal change and the longing for global change.

» That dangerous love and contagious hope should be the marks of the Body of Christ, breaking the church out of safety and comfort to radical engagement with those in need.

PEOPLE LIKE JESUS

In July 2007 Dr John Stott gave his last talk at the Keswick Convention. Entitled *The Model - Becoming More Like Christ*, the talk distilled the many years of Dr Stott's study, research and pastoral leadership to suggest one over-riding purpose for the people of God. We are called to become like Jesus. Dr Stott said:

I remember very vividly, some years ago, that the question which perplexed me as a younger Christian (and some of my friends as well) was this: what is God's purpose for his people? Granted that we have been converted, granted that we have been saved and received new life in Jesus Christ, what comes next? Of course, we knew the famous statement of the Westminster Shorter Catechism: that man's chief end is to glorify God and to enjoy him forever: we knew that, and we believed it. We also toyed with some briefer statements, like one of only five words – love God, love your neighbour. But somehow neither of these, nor some others that we could mention, seemed wholly satisfactory. So I want to share with you where my mind has come to rest as I approach the end of my pilgrimage on earth and it is – God wants his people to become like Christ. Christlikeness is the will of God for the people of God.

...we are to be like Christ in his mission. Having looked at the teaching of Paul and Peter, we come now to the teaching of Jesus recorded by John. In John 20:21, in prayer, Jesus said 'As you, Father, have sent me into the world, so I send them into the world' – that is us. And in his commissioning in John 17 he says 'As the Father sent me into the world, so I send you.' These words are immensely significant. This is not just the Johannine version of the Great Commission but it is also an instruction that their mission in the world was to resemble Christ's mission. In what respect? The key words in these texts are 'sent into the world'. As Christ has entered our world, so we are to enter other people's worlds. It was eloquently explained by Archbishop Michael Ramsey some years ago: 'We state and commend the faith only in so far as we go out and put ourselves with loving sympathy inside the doubts of the doubters, the questions of the questioners and the loneliness of those who have lost the way.' This entering into other people's worlds is exactly what we mean by incarnational evangelism. All authentic mission is incarnational mission. We are to be like Christ in his mission. [115]

BODY OF CHRIST

Stott's moving words, rich in wisdom and experience, connect with one of the New Testament's most frequently used images for the Church, as 'the body of Christ'. [116] When we see the Church described in these terms, we quite rightly see this as an image of unity and togetherness. The different 'members' of the one body work together towards the shared goals God has given. But there is more to this powerful and pervasive metaphor: it is also an image of incarnation. As Stott points out, we are called not only to reflect the identity of Christ in the world, but also to embody his mission.

There is a particular significance, in this light, of the fact that it is by baptism that we become part of God's Church. The symbolism of baptism identifies us directly with the life of Christ. Not only does our baptism emulate that of Christ in the River Jordan, but the very drama of his incarnation - the Son of God surrendering himself to live a human life, to die as humans die and to be raised victoriously to life - forms the basis of the journey we take in being baptised. The life of the Church is an incarnate, bodily life that we enter into by means of the thoroughly incarnate, bodily action of baptism.

The central celebration of the Church's life, the Eucharist, also celebrates the drama of Christ's incarnation. As we remember the brokenness of Christ's body, we remember that we, too, are one body, sharing in the one bread God has given us. We remember, too, that it was in self-giving love that God came to us. The Eucharistic meal is an honouring of the servant love that Christ has modelled for us, and calls us in turn to express.

115] Dr John Stott , *The Model – Becoming More Like Christ*, Keswick Convention, 17July 2007
116] Romans 12:4-6, 1 Corinthians 10:14-18, 1 Corinthians 12:12-31, Ephesians 1:23, 2:16, 3:6, 4:15, 5:23, 5:29, Colossians 1:18, 2:19, 3:18.

INCARNATE, INCARNATION, INCARNATIONAL

The word 'incarnate' simply means 'embodied' or 'in flesh'. It's most significant theological use is to describe the incarnation of Christ. This a specific event in history. In Jesus, God 'became flesh and blood and moved into the neighborhood'. [117] This is a unique event, a one-off moment in the history of salvation and according to C S Lewis the 'central miracle asserted by Christians.'[118] The Church cannot *repeat* the incarnation in this sense because it is made up of humans who are, by definition, flesh already. Neither do we *continue* or *replace* the incarnation of Christ, since we are told that Jesus has ascended bodily into heaven and having become human, is human forever. In this sense the Church is not called to *be* God incarnate, nor to *contain* or *continue* the incarnation of Christ. But the Church is, in a different sense, called to *incarnational* mission. We are called to imitate Christ in his servant love, to be his ongoing presence in the world and to continue in the world the ministry he has begun. To be the 'body of Christ' is to live out, in our own humanity, his mission of Jesus in the world.

CONTINUING PRESENCE

The language of 'body' was adopted by the apostles soon after Christ's own incarnation to suggest this sense that the Church is the continuing presence of Christ in the world, called to minister to those around us *just as Jesus would minister* to them were he here. The late Robert Webber wrote:

'The image of the Church as the body of Christ brings the other images together and puts the Church into an incarnational focus. The people of God who are a new creation, who share a common life together in Christ, constitute his body. Christ is still present in the world, no longer physically and literally, but spiritually and mystically in his body, the Church.' [119]

The Gospel-writer Luke, in his introduction to the book of Acts, implies this continuity. His first book (the Gospel of Luke) he suggests was about *'everything Jesus began to do and teach until the day he was taken up to heaven.'* [120] His second book (the Acts of the Apostles) he implies, will be about all that Jesus *continues* to do and teach through the Church. Stanley Grenz highlights the same link between the ministry of Jesus and that of the Church:

'Since his exaltation, the risen Lord continues his programme at the behest of the Father through the Holy Spirit who was poured out at Pentecost. This Spirit constitutes the Church as the body of Christ, whose ministry is the continuation of Christ's ministry.' [121]

This is a uncompromisingly communal metaphor: as individuals we may represent Jesus, but it is *as a body* that we become his presence in the world. Brian Walsh and Sylvia Keesmaat, in *Colossians Re:mixed*, describe a community that embodies a distinct and visible way of life inspired by the compassionate ministry of Jesus.

'What does a community renewed in knowledge according to the image of the Creator look like? It looks like the Creator. It *images* God. How? By embodying in its communal life the virtues that are formed by this God's story.' [122]

117] John 1:14, The Message
118] C S Lewis, *Miracles*, Harper One, 2001
119] Robert E Webber, *Common Roots: The Original Call to an Ancient-Future Faith*, Zondervan, 1978, 2009
120] Acts 1:1,2 NLT
121] Stanley J Grenz, *Theology for the Community of God*, Broadman and Holman,, 1994
122] Brian J Walsh and Sylvia C Keesmat, *Colossians Re:mixed: Subverting the Empire,* Paternoster, 2005, 2008

There is perhaps no clearer declaration of this call than that given by Paul to the Philippian Christians. Paul urges his Philippian friends to 'have the same attitude'[123] as Christ, describing for them the magnificent process by which Christ set aside power and possession to live for the service of others.[124] The beautiful words Paul cites here are believed to be part of a hymn or liturgy used by the first Christians. They constitute one of the earliest records we have of a Christian credal statement. Week by week the Christians assembled to celebrate Jesus and the life he had called them to. Brought together as his body, they in effect confessed, 'Christ poured himself out to serve others. We should do the same'.

Workout
Many Pixels, One Picture

*We often think of each believer being called to be like Jesus, and the What Would Jesus Do movement encourages this. But the body imagery of the New Testament is suggesting something slightly different - that **together**, as the Church, we make up a picture of Jesus. What difference is there for you between the phrases 'I should be like Jesus' and 'We should be like Jesus'? Does the thought of being one pixel, rather than trying to be the whole picture, help you?*

Speaker's Corner
The Best and Worst of the Church
Viv Thomas

What do you love most about the Church?
I travel around the world four months every year and the Church is more adorable, more beautiful and more stunning than the Grand Canyon, Table Mountain or the mighty Ganges put together in one place. The Church is the most beautiful thing I know.

What do you struggle with most about the Church?
I struggle with particular churches when they are overcome by fear, curl up into a ball, close their eyes, put their fingers in each ear and congeal into their final static shut down shape.

NEW ORDER

Servant love, in reflection of Christ, was the earliest mark of this revolutionary community, and remains to this day God's call to us. We are invited not only to receive the grace and mercy of God in Jesus, but to be ministers of that grace and mercy in the world. To feed on the bread of life and with the bread of life feed the world. [125]

ROBERT WEBBER WRITES

The 'body' image of the Church is not a mere organisation of human persons, but a new revolutionary society of people... As a new order, a new humanity, the Church has always had within it the power to be an explosive force in society and in the history of the world. For it is called not to *contain* its message but to live and to proclaim its message, calling all people into a repentance from the old body, the old humanity, the old creation, Satan's kingdom, the former age into the new body, the new humanity, the new creation, the new kingdom, the new age. [126]

As Hans Küng expresses it:

'The Church exists for the world by being committed to the world ... If it truly follows its Lord, the Church is called to active service of its brethren, who are all created by the one Father. A church which only lived and worked for itself would not be the Church of Christ.'[127]

Ephesians 4 encourages us to see this link between the 'body' imagery of the Church and the call to service. Paul sets the equipping of God's people for service (4:12) in the context of the Church as Christ's body (4:4). We are a body in unity and a body in action!

123] Philippians 2:5
124] Philippians 2:6-11
125] John 6:51
126] Robert E Webber, *Common Roots: The Original Call to an Ancient-Future Faith*, Zondervan, 1978, 2009
127] Hans Küng, *The Church*, Continuum, 2001

SERVANT REVOLUTION

The incarnation of Christ, as expressed in Philippians 2, is revolutionary in that it moves *counter to* the expectations of history. God's descent into humanity is unexpected, contradicting the norms of privilege and power. This revolutionary love models for the Church a calling that will also run counter to cultural expectation. Bryan Stone writes:

> The Church that is called to reach and engage the world should not be surprised to find itself also living in contradiction to that world ... The most evangelistic thing the Church can do, therefore, is to be the Church not merely *in* public but as a new and alternative public; not merely *in* society but as a new and distinct society, a new and unprecedented social existence. [128]

There is evidence in recent years, perhaps especially among the rising generations, that the rediscovery of the call to a 'servant revolution' has been a significant step of faith for many believers. For many young adults this is a primary test of the authenticity of faith. Where *right doctrine* was for earlier generations the litmus test of belonging, *right living* or *right loving* has become, for many, paramount. As we wrestle with what it means to be the body of Christ in our postmodern, post-Christendom society, is there a particular need for us to discover what a community of 'embodied love' might look like? To embrace this incarnational call and see our identity as the body of Christ not just as a call to unity but also as a call to action, will highlight for us three key aspects of God's purpose for the Church:

» To be the body of Christ is to embody love. To be the body of Christ means not only to be united, but also to be in some sense the presence of Christ in the world. Faithful to the character of Christ, we continue his ministry and presence.

» To be the body of Christ is to look to the transformation of the world. Acts of servant love bring transformation to our world - personally, relationally, socially and globally. It is through love that God changes us, and through love that he will change the world.

» To be the body of Christ is to embrace the poor. In God's plans for the world, there is a special place for the poor and broken. Those whose lives most demonstrate the absence of God's peace will be the first to know when God's peace comes. The Church is called to show love to the poor - in its community and in the world.

128] Bryan P Stone, *Evangelism After Christendom: The Theology and Practice of Christian Witness*, Brazos Press, 2006

EMBODYING LOVE
WE ARE CALLED TO IMITATE CHRIST
IN HIS SERVANT LOVE:
EMBODYING HIS MERCY IN THE WORLD

God is love, the Bible teaches us. God in Christ is love incarnate. Our participation in Christ is essentially a call to love. [129] The more we love, the more we reflect God. Stanley Grenz writes:

'As the people united together, God calls us to exemplify in the midst of the brokenness of the present, the eschatological ideal community of love, which is the divine essence. The Church is to be the fellowship of individuals who are bound together by the love present among them through the power of God's Spirit which is exemplified by humble service to each other and the world. Indeed, as we exist in love, we reflect what God is like.' [130]

To embody Christ is to embody love. Wherever the body of Christ is present, love should be found, so that the very act of creating and growing churches is an act of embodying love. According to church-planter Steve Taylor, this is the essence of Church.

'In John 1, the Word is made flesh and moves into the neighbourhood. This enfleshed Word forms a community, a group of people. The community embodies the redemptive love of God. Then in John 20:21 the sending Jesus breathes on this community. They receive the Spirit and are sent, as Jesus was sent. And so the task of being disciples is to *form communities that embody redemptive trinitarian love.* The planting of embodied communities is essential to the mission of God ... Being the body of God is essential to redemptive community.' [131]

The 16th century mystic Teresa of Avila captured this sense of embodied love in a much-quoted poem: *Christ Has No Body*

Christ has no body but yours,
No hands, no feet on earth but yours,
Yours are the eyes with which he looks
With compassion on this world,
Yours are the feet with which he walks to do good,
Yours are the hands, with which he blesses all the world.
Yours are the hands, yours are the feet,
Yours are the eyes, you are his body.
Christ has no body now on earth but yours. [132]

129] 1 John 4:7-9
130] Stanley J Grenz, *Theology for the Community of God*, Broadman and Holman, 1994
131] Steve Taylor, *The Out of Bounds Church: Learning to Create a Community of Faith in a Culture of Change*, Youth Specialities, 2005
132] Teresa of Avila (1515–1582), *The Journey with Jesus: Poems and Prayers,* selected by Dan Clendenin
http://www.journeywithjesus.net/PoemsAndPrayers/Teresa_Of_Avila_Christ_Has_No_Body.shtml

Workout
Christ is Love

The preceeding paragraphs make the assumption that to embody Christ is to embody love. Only a community of love can genuinely be described as the Body of Christ, and it is in acts of servant love that the Church shows itself to be Christ's body. Do you agree with this? If so, how does this impact your priorities and goals as a Church?

Theologians have questioned the poem's over-emphasis on a 'repeated' incarnation, but it delivers nonetheless a significant message: it is *through the Church* that Christ continues to minister in the world. In his earthly ministry Jesus touched people not only metaphorically but physically - he healed, more often than not, through *touch*. It is in this sense that we are called to continue his work. There are other senses in which God is at work in the world: by his sovereign decision and in the operations of common grace. But there are specific and substantial ways in which it is *through the Church* that God touches the world. As James Bryan Smith asserts:

'[God's] love can and must extend itself through our own hands and feet, expressed in our love for others. We were created for a purpose. Not simply to wait until we die and go to heaven, but created 'in Christ Jesus for good works.' [133]

Workout
God Con Carne

A familiar term derived, via Spanish, from the Latin term 'caro' is Chilli Con Carne - literally chillies with meat. Is it too graphic a step to speak of God incarnate as God in meat? God incarnate is not an idea but a person; visible and concrete; able to touch and be touched. So love incarnate can never be simply an idea or a word: it must be visible and concrete, something that can touch and be touched. It is in this sense that the Church continues the incarnate ministry of Christ.

THE TRUTH IN LOVE

The love of God becomes incarnate again when it is expressed in acts of love by the Church. We talk of 'reaching' or 'touching' the world, but we forget how *physical* these words are. Linguist Alison Morgan writes:

'When Paul tells the Ephesian church to 'speak the truth in love', the verb he uses in fact means not just to *speak* the truth but rather to do, to *maintain*, to *live* the truth. And that is our task too. Of ourselves, we can change nothing. But when we speak and live the truth, we find that our words and our deeds have the power of God himself.' [134]

Love, then, is essential to what it means to be the body of Christ. Love is, as Francis Schaeffer wrote, 'the mark of the Christian'.

'Only with this mark may the world know that Christians are indeed Christians and that Jesus was sent by the Father.' [135]

In this sense, Schaeffer asserts, the love of the Church *validates* the incarnation. To put the same argument in the reverse form, how many people have questioned the incarnation of Christ because they have not found love in his representative community, the Church? How many would find their experience reflected in that of emerging church-planter Joe Boyd, who writes:

'I read the Gospels over and over. Nothing I was doing on Sunday was what I thought Jesus would be doing if he were here.' [136]

Just as God communicated love for humanity not by sending words but by sending his son, so now he communicates love through the visible, embodied, presence of the Church. As Lesslie Newbigin says,

'It is surely a fact of inexhaustible significance that what our Lord left behind him was not a book, nor a creed, nor a system of thought, nor a rule of life, but a visible community ... He committed the entire work of salvation to that community.' [137]

133] James Bryan Smith, *The Good and Beautiful Community*, Hodder and Stoughton, 2010
134] Alison Morgan, *The Wild Gospel*, extract at http://www.fulcrum-anglican.org.uk/page.cfm?ID=252
135] Francis Schaeffer, *The Mark of the Christian*, IVP Classics, 2006
136] Joe Boyd, Apex, *Las Vegas*, cited in Eddie Gibbs and Ryan K Bolger, *Emerging Churches: Creating Christian Community in Postmodern Cultures*, Baker Academic, 2005
137] Lesslie Newbigin, *The Household of God*, SCM, 1953; Paternoster, 1998

HOPEquotes: People of HOPE

'OVER **60** CHURCHES, PART OF HOPE CALDERDALE, ADDRESS LOCAL NEEDS BY BACKING OUR FOOD AND SUPPORT DROP-IN. CLIENTS ARE HELPED TO MOVE ON FROM SITUATIONS LIKE HOMELESSNESS OR ADDICTION AND MANY NOW REQUEST PRAYER TOO. WE ARE JUST PEOPLE OF HOPE WITH A DESIRE FOR OTHERS TO KNOW THAT A NEW LIFE IS AVAILABLE THROUGH JESUS.' [138]

LOVE IS LIVED

This love, lived out by the people of God, is the essence of his mission in the world. Through embodied love, the community of faith in its very life *announces* and *anticipates* God's loving purposes for the planet. Vinay Samuel writes:

Through word, sacrament and action, and in its own corporate life, the congregation is to make clear God's loving purpose to heal and reconcile humankind to God in Jesus Christ. The congregation is called to be an inclusive, risk-taking community, practising hospitality learned from God's graciousness and embracing the excluded in the way of Christ. In faithfulness to the apostolic mission of the Church, the congregation is called to issue an invitation. The Holy Spirit is active in the Church, but also outside the Church. So mission includes caring for and affirming God's redeeming love for all creation. [139]

This 'living out' of God's love should not be seen as a 'task' or 'function' of the Church. We cannot love others as a duty. It is, rather, the overflow of God's love for us. The community of love established in the Church is, first and foremost, the community of God's love for us. It is through participation in the life of God in this community that I first know myself as loved, and it is only when I know myself as loved that I can even begin to love others. Living out such a love then calls me to move outwards, towards those I am seeking to love. There is an an impulse to 'move into the neighbourhood' just as Christ has done. Embodiment cannot remain detached from those it loves - it seeks contact. One of the measures of incarnation is proximity. As the Catholic Church expressed in the findings of the Second Vatican Council:

'If the Church is to be in a position to offer all men the mystery of salvation and the life brought by God, then it must implant itself among all these groups in the same way that Christ by his incarnation committed himself to the particular social and cultural circumstances of the men among whom he lived.' [140]

This love, though, is not a question of 'doing' but of 'being'. Love will never be seen in what we 'do' until it is the very basis of what we are.

138] Kate Fawcett, Food and Support Drop-in, Halifax
139] Vinay Samuel, cited in Chris Sugden, *Gospel, Culture and Transformation*, Regnum Books, 1997 and 2000
140] From the Decree on the Church's Missionary Activity of the Second Vatican Council, Ad Gentes 10 in Austin Flannery (ed.), *Vatican Council II; The Conciliar and Post Conciliar Documents*, Costello Publishing Company, 1988

Workout
Carriers of Love

What kind of community does the Church need to be to embody in this way God's love for all people, and to carry that love to every corner of the world?

The call to love and serve our communities applies to every church in every setting - it is not just for large urban or suburban congregations to take-on. The conditions of the rural Church illustrate how local context impacts the Church's mission. Sally Gaze, Team Rector of a rural benefice and Chair of the Fresh Expressions Rural Round Table, suggests that rural churches may be shaped in their mission by a number of factors:

» **Small numbers** - the body of Christ is truly diverse and we know each other well enough to truly feel for each other, but it is not always possible in to run separate programmes for different age groups within a single congregation. Such programmes may only be possible if they cover a wide geographical area and are supported by several churches in partnership.

» **Lay ministry** - one paid minister for many, dispersed (small) congregations means that every member ministry is usually a reality. Sometimes this leads to lay leaders being less mature in their faith than you might wish - and sometimes it leads to people growing very fast!

» **Buildings** - often the church building will be the last community building in a village to remain open. The village may regard the church as 'theirs' even if they don't attend. This presents both challenges and opportunities for mission.

» **Restricted funding** - smaller congregations mean less income, and rural churches may not be able to afford or access high tech resources. For some churches high tech would mean access to electric light or running water in buildings! Simple can be beautiful, but programmes and worship styles have to be adapted - the latest urban or suburban initiative will not play easily in many settings.

» **Neighbours** - in small communities, everyone may know everyone - our lives are very visible to our neighbours.

» **Change** - the rural context is undergoing very fast social change, with the break up of communities causing distress. Many who have been raised in the countryside are unable to afford to live there in young adulthood.

Some of these factors will also be true of smaller urban and suburban congregations, but it remains true that the rural context calls for specific and particular ministry approaches.

Speaker's Corner
The Best and Worst of the Church
Andy Hickford

What do you love most about the Church?

What do you struggle with most about the Church?

people

people

TRANSFORMING THE WORLD

Love brings change, and the love of Christ in us can change the world

For missiologist Alan Hirsch the love of God embodied in the Church is more than a simple attribute of community: it is a seed with world-changing potential. He writes:

'In some mysterious way, when we are incorporated into God's family, we all seem to become 'seeds' bearing the full potential of the God's people within us. If you or I were blown like a seed into a different field, God could create a Jesus community out of both of us. This is the marvel of a true people movement. And where it is unleashed and cultivated, world transformation takes place.' [141]

Transformation has become for many the most effective category in which to understand God's purposes for the Church. David Bosch's now classic work *Transforming Mission* [142] has introduced a whole generation to this context, leading to some of the most creative thinking of recent decades on Church and mission. Transformation connects the Church of God to the mission of God. It is the goal towards which we express Christ's love: the ultimate purpose of being 'the body of Christ'.

Graham Tomlin, in *The Provocative Church*, suggests that:

'A healthy Church is a transforming community in both senses. It is a community that transforms those who belong to it, loosing the hold of our addiction to sin, and replacing it with a love for what is good and healthy, every bit as much as an AA meeting tries practically to loose the hold of alcohol on its members, replacing it with something better. It also transforms the life of the community around it in slow but sure ways.' [143]

'Transformation is at the heart of God's mission to humanity', Ed Stetzer and Thom Rainer suggest:

'He delights in moving us from the kingdom of darkness to the kingdom of light - and then empowering and directing us as agents of his kingdom. And he has chosen the Church as his instrument in this world. We, the Body of Christ, are God's chosen method to deliver the message of transformation to our neighbours, both in the local community and around the world.' [144]

CHANGED PEOPLE CHANGE PEOPLE

Transformation builds the bridge between the *spiritual formation* experienced by the individual and the *mission of God* embodied by the Church. As we are changed inwardly by the Spirit, so we join God in changing the world. What the Spirit begins *in us* he continues *through us* in the world. Changed people change people, and the people they change, change the world.

141] Alan Hirsch, *The Forgotten Ways: Reactivating the Missional Church*, Brazos Press, 2006
142] David J Bosch,*Transforming Mission: Paradigm Shifts in Theology of Mission*, Orbis, 1991
143] Graham Tomlin, *The Provocative Church*, SPCK, 2002 and 2004
144] Ed Stetzer and Thom S Rainer, *Transformational Church*, B and H Publishing Group and Lifeway Research, 2010

Workout
Transformers

*Graham Tomlin suggests that 'a healthy Church is a transforming community' and Ed Stetzer and Thom Rainer claim that 'transformation is at the heart of God's mission'. Is this something you have seen at work in your own local setting? Is **change** - inwardly and outwardly, the mark of your Christian experience? If it is not, what steps can you take to move towards a 'transforming' faith? How can the ordinary members of a local church sensitively influence their community of faith in this direction?*

ENGAGEMENT NOT RETREAT

Transformation is a recipe for engagement with the world. It calls the Church to dive head-first into human cultures, declaring and demonstrating the revolutionary love of Christ. As Al Hirsch and Lance Ford express it:

'Contrary to many of the images of the Church as a defensive fortress, suffering the terrible, relentless onslaughts of hell, the movement that Jesus set in motion is designed to be an advancing, untamed, and untamable revolutionary force created to transform the world.' [145]

'What is mission?', Roger Greenacre asks, 'If not the engagement with God in the entire enterprise of bringing the whole of creation to its intended destiny?'[146] As Ed Stetzer and Thom Rainer suggest:

'Gospel change has always led to broader change. The gospel's power reaches into all nooks and crannies, soaks into all places, plants seeds, and bears fruit.' [147]

For many churches looking to engage with contemporary Western culture, embracing the goal of social transformation has been a sea-change in understanding mission. Embodying the love of Christ opens the Church to a broader, richer tapestry than the concerns of individual salvation: though these remain as part of the picture. The Bible speaks of a future in which all creation will be transformed, liberated from the bondage of sin, [148] and in acts of embodied love the Church lives out, here and now, that future. Churches with a focus on the promised future, Reggie McNeal suggests, are seeing transformation as 'the crux of the matter':

'Churches that understand the realities of the present future are shifting the target of ministry efforts from church activity to community transformation. This is turning the Church inside out.' [149]

145] Alan Hirsch and Lance Ford, *Right Here Right Now: Everyday Mission for Everyday People*, Baker Books, 2011
146] Robin Greenwood, *Practising Community*, SPCK, 1996, p. 28. cited in Mission Shaped Church, Church House, 2004
147] Robin Greenwood, *Practising Community*, SPCK, 1996, p. 28. cited in Mission Shaped Church, Church House, 2004
148] Romans 8:19-27
149] Reggie McNeal, *The Present Future: Six Tough Questions for the Church*, Jossey Bass, 2003

So What?
Measuring Change

Many family homes have a cupboard door somewhere with a number of different heights marked on it, showing the growth, over the years, of the children. If you had a similar system to show the transformation brought about in your community by your Church, what changes would you mark? Are there measures, apart from attendance numbers, to show the progress, or otherwise, of your Church? What do you think transformation should look like in your local context?

Through embodied love the Church participates in God's transformation of the world. Vinay Samuel writes:

Transformation is to enable God's vision of society to be actualised in all relationships; social, economic and spiritual, so that God's will may be reflected in human society and his love be experienced by all communities, especially the poor. [150]

To be the Body of Christ then, is to live-out the principles of Christ's incarnation. In its internal relationships and in its external impact, the Church is called to be a community of embodied love - with servanthood and sacrifice written through it like 'Brighton' through a stick of rock.

Workout
Power to the Poor

Vinay Samuel suggests above that kingdom transformation will particularly impact on the lives of the poor. Is this what you see in the UK Church? If not, what steps or actions would make this more evident among us?

150] Vinay Samuel, cited in Chris Sugden, *Gospel, Culture and Transformation*, Regnum Books, 1997 and 2000

DANGEROUS LOVE
Patrick Regan

As I walked through an estate with the local vicar, he told me of a generation of young people living here who have never known their parents to have a job - the prospect of a future that includes a job is seen as an unachievable goal.

Persistent poverty makes you angry, especially when you grow up in a city where deprivation exists in such close proximity to wealth and prosperity – often only a road away. Combined with issues such as family breakdown, poor housing, educational failure, and the problems of drugs and crime in their neighbourhoods, many children and young people can find themselves unloved, unwanted, and with no sense of belonging or hope for the future. Often their behaviours and attitudes alienate them from their own families and communities. Many end up excluded from school and embrace the twisted and distorted sense of family offered through gangs, becoming outcasts from society.
Amy said to me,

'The gangs I joined seemed the only people in the world to offer a kind of comfort and caring. The desire to feel wanted, in a world that seems to regard me as scum, was very powerful.'

Another kid, Si, said, 'Eight years old! That's when my life went downhill. From eight years old no one looked after me. I just lived on the streets and made do by myself.' Until Si was eight years old, his life was great. With five sisters and parents who adored him, he was happy, safe and secure. But that all changed one day when, with no warning or explanation, his mother left the country taking his sisters with her. His dad could not cope and sent Si to live with his elderly grandma. Can you imagine what that must be like for an eight-year-old child? Si now faces many years of rehab ahead of him if he is ever to walk or talk again since being shot in the head in a gang incident. [151]

Life for Amy and Si, and thousands like them, who live in our inner-city estates, is about to become even worse with the looming financial cuts; the poorest and the most marginalised will feel it most.

The question is: how are we going to respond? Often, when times are difficult and uncertain, our instinct is to pull up the drawbridge, baton down the hatches, and look after ourselves. But you see, I feel that every Christian and congregation is called to be so much more – we are called to be courageous, to be outrageously generous towards to poor, to give not only of our finances but of ourselves to the point where it hurts – and then to give even more.

Isaiah 58 sees the people asking to receive blessings from God, yet they are arguing amongst themselves and they are complaining their sacrifices have not been accepted. Isaiah the prophet steps in and tells them what to do if they want God to accept their sacrifices:

What I'm interested in seeing you do is: sharing your food with the hungry, inviting the homeless poor into your homes, putting clothes on the shivering ill-clad, being available to your own families. [152]

And what happens when we are like this? 'Hope'. When we are courageous, generous and giving to the point where it hurts, 'Hope,' even in the most overwhelming of situations, is the result. When a mother rings our office, in tears on the phone, to thank our workers for the positive change she's seen in the son whom she feared would become involved in gangs and crime,

hope becomes contagious. Their story gets told and retold. It becomes what Michael Frost calls a 'dangerous story!'[153] Why dangerous? Because it has the power to change lives, futures, and even eternities.

Isaiah challenges us to be courageous, outrageously generous and to give everything. As we embrace the poor and the marginalised, stories begin to be told, powerful and dangerous stories that would change the course of human history and the destiny of believers. Isaiah 58 calls out to God's people over the centuries to be the same.

How amazing and dangerous would Amy's story have been, if she had said to me, 'The church I joined seemed to be the only people in the world to offer comfort and caring. The desire to feel wanted, in a world that seems to regard me as scum, was very powerful.' And Isaiah 58 says, when we become like this, God makes us a dangerous promise:
'Then when you pray, God will answer...You'll be known as those who can fix anything, restore old ruins, rebuild and renovate, make the community liveable again.' [154]

How dangerous are we prepared to become; dangerous enough to make a difference?

Patrick Regan, CEO, XLP
www.xlp.org.uk

151] P Regan, Fighting Chance, Tackling Britain's Gang Culture, Hodder, 2010 p56
152] Isaiah 58, The Message
153] SM Frost., Exiles, Living Missionally in a Post-Christian Culture, Hendrickson, 2006
154] Isaiah 58, The Message

EMBRACING THE POOR

God loves the poor and his desire is to love the poor through us

St Francis of Assisi accounts for his love of the poor in a famous incident in which he found himself 'kissing the leper'. In his novel *Chasing Francis,* Ian Morgan Cron records a similar life-changing moment. The novel explores the life and spirituality of Francis through that of troubled mega-church pastor Chase Falson. At a climactic moment in the book, Falcon is taken by a Franciscan sister to help in an Aids hospice. He is asked to bathe the emaciated and fragile body of a dying patient. In the moment of caring for this broken and helpless man, he experiences God's love overwhelmingly. When his travelling companion later asks 'What happened up there?', Falson - a long-term church-planter and successful Pastor - says 'I think I became a Christian'. [155]

Incarnational ministry, it seems, has a special place for the poor. As we embody the love of Christ for the world and join with God in its transformation, we find ourselves drawn towards those in greatest need. Stanley Grenz writes:

'Christ has called us to a ministry of service. But what is this task? Following Jesus example leads us to a ministry of service that focusses on meeting the needs of the less-fortunate of the world. Like the good Samaritan, we bind up the wounds of the injured and outcast of the world.' [156]

An account of the ministry of the Body of Christ that leaves out this emphasis on the poor is neither biblical nor complete. Incarnation points us toward compassion: literally to 'suffer with' those in need. [157] Richard Stearns, now CEO of World Vision, describes our failure to engage with the poor as 'the hole in our gospel'. He writes:

'If your personal faith in Christ has no positive outward expression, then your faith - and mine - has a hole in it ... Embracing the gospel, or good news, proclaimed by Jesus is so much more than a private transaction between God and us. The gospel itself was born of God's vision of a changed people, challenging and transforming the prevailing values and practices of our world ... Jesus asked a great deal of those who followed him. He expected much more from them than just believing he was God's son. He challenged them to embrace radically different standards, to love their neighbours *and* their enemies, to forgive those who wronged them, to lift up the poor and downtrodden, to share what they had with those who had little, and to live lives of sacrifice.' [158]

SHALOM CHURCH

One way of understanding this emphasis on the poor is to understand the Bible's emphasis on peace. Peace, *shalom* in Hebrew, is more than the absence of war. It is well-being; health. It can mean both wholeness of body and harmony in relationships. [159] It is the evidence of God's blessing.[160] Where *shalom* is absent, God the peace-maker moves in. Jesus, God's Messiah, is the Prince of Peace,[161] who comes to declare *'Glory to God in the highest heaven, and on earth peace...'* [162] In incarnation Christ comes from heaven *'to shine on those living in darkness and in the shadow of death, to guide our feet into the path of peace.'* [163] Of those who will follow him, Jesus says, *'Blessed are the peacemakers, for they will be called children of God'* [164] Peter is later able to summarise the gospel as *'the good news of peace through Jesus Christ'.* [165] Paul refers repeatedly to the peace found in Christ and, in Ephesians, describes Jesus as the one who *'preached peace to you who were far away and peace to those who were near'.*[166] The gospel, then, is the restoration of *shalom*, and it is where *shalom* is most absent that the gospel is most needed. The poor; the broken; the victims of injustice and abuse; the trapped; the imprisoned: those most in need of the good news of peace will, by definition, be 'targets' of God's love. Where the kingdom comes, *shalom* is restored, and where *shalom* is restored, the kingdom has come. Craig Nessan, in *Shalom Church*, writes:

155] Ian Morgan Cron, *Chasing Francis: A Pilgrim's Tale*, NavPress, 2006
156] Stanley J Grenz, *Theology for the Community of God*, Broadman and Holman, 1994
157] http://oxforddictionaries.com/definition/compassion
158] Richard Stearns, *The Hole in Our Gospel: What Does God Expect of Us? The Answer that Changed my Life and Might Just Change the World*, World Vision, 2009
159] http://www.biblestudytools.com/dictionaries/bakers-evangelical-dictionary/peace.html
160] Numbers 6:26
161] Isaiah 9:6
162] Luke 2:14
163] Luke 1:79
164] Matthew 5:9
165] Acts 10:36
166] Ephesians 2:17

'God is calling the Church as the body of Christ to act as a servant for the mending of creation ... By giving itself away to nourish a world in need, the Church discovers its vocation as a ministering community ... In discovering Jesus in the faces and bodies of the world's lost and forsaken ones and by ministering to him there, the Church discovers its deep gladness.' [167]

The call of the Church to participate in the 'mending of creation' also reminds us that the love God calls us to show is not exclusively a love for his human creatures: it is a love for the whole creation. Churches refer often to the 'great commission' of Matthew 28, calling us to make disciples, but there is also a 'First Commission' in scripture, centuries before this. It comes not in the Gospels but in Genesis, and is the calling to Adam and Eve to care for the whole creation, 'husbanding' the animals and plants of God's garden. To truly enter into God's plans for the Church, then, is to show servant love to the whole creation. Can we include 'caring for God's earth' as an explicit aspect of the mission God calls us to?

Workout

Peace vs No Peace

*Shalom is the presence of God's peace. Where God's peace has not come, there is no **shalom**. Draw a line down the middle of a blank piece of paper and write 'Know Peace' and 'No Peace' across the top, as shown below. Under each, and for each of the following areas of life and culture, describe what the presence or absence of God's peace looks like:*

	Know Peace	No Peace
Politics		
Economy		
Young People		
Arts		
Media		

167] Craig L Nessan, *Shalom Church: The Body of Christ as Ministering Community*, Fortress Press, 2010

INTEGRAL MISSION

Missiologists use the term 'integral mission' to describe this wider calling of the Church. The Micah declaration on integral mission, for example, states that:

'It is not simply that evangelism and social involvement are to be done along side each other. Rather, in integral mission, our proclamation has social consequences as we call people to love and repentance in all areas of life. And our social involvement has evangelistic consequences as we bear witness to the transforming grace of Jesus Christ. If we ignore the world, we betray the word of God which sends us out to serve the world. If we ignore the word of God, we have nothing to bring to the world. *Justice and justification by faith, worship and political action, the spiritual and the material, personal change and structural change belong together.* As in the life of Jesus, being, doing and saying are at the heart of our integral task.' [168]

Development agency Tearfund defines integral mission as 'the work of the Church in contributing to the positive physical, spiritual, economic, psychological and social transformation of people.' [169]

So What?
Integral Mission

The definition of 'integral mission' used by Tearfund has been arrived at through many years of working with churches in developing nations. Where extreme poverty is self-evident, the Church has understood its responsibility to function in both the spiritual and the material dimensions. But what about the home front? How does integral mission play out in your local setting? If you made a commitment as a church to address the 'physical, spiritual, economic, psychological' needs of your community, what would the first steps be of shaping your strategy?

For a church congregation, the challenge is to ask how such an integral approach plays out in the local setting. How does a local church express its commitment to justice and justification; to personal transformation *and* social change? How do the activities we promote and sponsor, the prayers we pray and the cycles of worship we design reflect an integral understanding of God's mission in the world?

WALKING *WITH* NOT TALKING *TO...*

Bryant Myers describes this ministry not as action done 'to the poor' but as 'walking with the poor'. [170] Embodied love comes alongside those in need. It stands with the poor. Spencer Burke recounts his discovery of this truth in an unusual encounter with the police:

On one occasion, our community was getting kicked out of a park because of our interaction with the homeless. 'You can't feed the homeless here; you need a permit,' the policeman said. I replied, 'We are not feeding the homeless. We are having a picnic. We're eating *with* them.' [171]

'I see Jesus in those in need' Tony Campolo says, 'If I did not have that foundation, my caring for them would be of no value. It would be pity, and no-one wants to be pitied. I see Christ in them, and I love them. That is why I do what I do. [172]

168] http://tilz.tearfund.org/Churches/What+is+integral+mission.htm
169] http://tilz.tearfund.org/webdocs/Tilz/Churches/0.4.1%20Tearfunds%20definition%20of%20integral%20mission.pdf
170] Bryant L Myers, *Walking With the Poor: Principles and Practices of Transformational Development*, Orbis, 1999
171] Spencer Burke, cited in Eddie Gibbs and Ryan K Bolger, *Emerging Churches: Creating Christian Community in Postmodern Cultures*, Baker Academic, 2005
172] Tony Campolo, cited in James Bryan Smith, *The Good and Beautiful Community*, Hodder and Stoughton, 2010

LARK IN THE PARK

New Generation Church has always played an active role in the community of Sidcup, in South East London, and began to recognise the growing need to build community, create a central gathering to connect the local residents and ultimately, share the gospel with an increasingly busy and private commuter town.

A handful of people in the church took on the challenge of bridging this gap by creating and delivering a free, two-week community festival, and in 1996, Lark in the Park was founded with a couple of tents and some live music.

Today, Lark in the Park attracts around 1,500 people a day, and puts on events, activities and clubs tailor-made to suit the varying age ranges of the visitors. In 2004, Churches Together in Sidcup began to support the event and now volunteers from over 20 different churches, locally and further-a–field, work alongside each other to deliver a varied programme including vibrant children's clubs, culturally relevant youth events and action teams, who serve the local community off-site in practical and measurable ways.

This practical outworking of local churches unified in mission is displayed every morning when volunteers meet in the big top for 'Connections' – a time of worship, testimony and teaching. This has become the daily call to mission, inspiring and empowering hundreds of volunteers simply to demonstrate the love of God through serving the visitors that come to the event. In this equipping meeting, volunteers are encouraged to pray and invite the presence of God before heading off to their teams and putting it into practice.

The Lark in the Park team firmly believes in Holy Spirit-led evangelism and daily they collect prayer requests from members of the public. The team even take prayer out into the park in the form of 'Park Pastors', who not only serve tea and coffee to the crowds of people enjoying the live entertainment and music on the Park Life centre stage, but offer prayer to individuals. Regularly they have opportunities to pray for people's healing, encouragement and other needs.

Inevitably in fifteen years of Lark in the Park, there have been lessons learned along the journey and Paul Weston, Leader of New Generation Church and Event Leader of Lark in the Park, recognises the importance of releasing creativity in team leaders and volunteers. Some time ago, one particular individual expressed an interest in creating an event for the more elderly visitors to the park. Today the 'Freedom Zone' offers afternoon tea, live music performances and hand massages, for the hundreds of over 60s that visit each week. Over 20 people made a commitment to God during one of their afternoon gatherings.

As Lark in the Park has developed, the team steering the event reiterate the importance of avoiding 'hit and run evangelism' and instead, creating and building community. This is told in the story of a local resident who first noticed the event banner whilst driving past the park. After checking out the festival for herself, she began to volunteer on team, teaching salsa dancing, and later, made a personal commitment to God.

This year, a record 420 volunteers were mobilised to serve the local community, some, on team for the first time since making a commitment to God in response to their visit last year.

In a park in a South London borough, where bankers, journalists, teachers, parents, medical professionals and teenagers alike are equipped and released to demonstrate God's love to the general public through service, Lark in the Park showcases the impact that can be made on a community when the people of God are empowered by the Church.

For more information on Lark in the Park, visit www.larkinthepark.com

Workout
With Not To

*What is the difference between ministering **to** the poor and those in need and sharing life **with** the poor and those in need? What actions by a church make the difference between a 'to the poor' and a 'with the poor' orientation?*

RISING BROOK AND INDIA'S DALITS

Malcolm Egner tells the story of his own journey with mission amongst the poor, and how a mainstream Baptist pastor become a champion of freedom for some of the world's most disadvantaged people:

I am a minister at Rising Brook Baptist Church in Stafford. Until five years ago, I had never heard the word 'Dalit'. I was at a conference and heard about how these 250 million people were oppressed and marginalised, the victims of discrimination and atrocities simply because they fell below India's rigid caste system. In the space of five minutes I was changed. My heart broke as I heard about the reality of life as a Dalit – an untouchable – in India today. Later that year I went with a friend from church and spent a week visiting schools and other projects that are helping to lift Dalits out of poverty and exploitation – a response to the request for help from Dalit leaders. It was an eye-opening experience.

Following on from this visit, our church agreed to partner with a church movement in India by sending teams to resource a series of family conferences – for pastors, men and women, children and youth workers – in the city of Pune and the state of Maharashtra. For the last four years, teams of 15-25 people of all ages have taken part in what is a life-changing experience. Our report-back sessions are very moving, as members of the team describe how their visit has made a strong impact on their life and faith. They have been used in ways they never thought possible. For the Dalit Christians we met, they have been deeply moved by (mainly) white British people treating them with honour and dignity – sitting, eating, queuing, communicating, praying and holding hands with them.

Three years ago, an Indian leader, Dr Joseph D'Souza, visited Rising Brook. He spoke about how extreme poverty and discrimination makes Dalits particularly vulnerable to trafficking and bonded labour. They make up almost half of all those in slavery around the world today. Joseph spoke about his desire to address the issue by tackling the traffickers and caring for the victims and survivors. As he spoke, something stirred in my heart, again.

In response to this challenge, the church's Justice Issues group asked 'How can we support you in this struggle?'. From initially imagining people lending their help through professional skills, time and finance, the answer became something on a much bigger scale. I realised that it would need someone who was able to give more than their spare time, and perhaps God was calling me to change my life's direction. As a result, Rising Brook was involved in setting up a human rights organisation, Dalit Freedom Network UK, and I was seconded half-time to head up the campaign to end Dalit trafficking.

On our fact-finding trip we met with Devadasi – Dalit women who had been dedicated to a goddess as young girls, then sold for sex on reaching puberty. Many are trafficked, most are trapped in sex slavery. In response to this ritualised prostitution, and to the other forms of slavery faced by Dalits – trafficking for sex, bonded labour (debt bondage), child beggar gangs, marriage, domestic service and the harvesting of body parts – members of Rising Brook have set in motion a campaign to lobby Parliament, raise awareness through Dalit Freedom Champions and Action Groups across the UK, and support on-the-ground anti-trafficking projects in India – refuge shelters, education, healthcare, economic development, women's empowerment.

Through this work, Dalits have been rescued from trafficking, and many are being lifted out of the cycle of poverty and exploitation. Communities are being transformed. The Dalit Freedom Network works with people of many faiths, but it has been a Christian community that has been the catalyst for the campaign, and now people from across the UK are getting involved to make a real difference. [173]

Speaker's Corner
The Best and Worst of the Church
Simon Hall

What do you love most about the Church?
I love the people! I'm so glad I'm not alone in this, and that I am surrounded by friends who support me and are strong when I am weak.

What do you struggle with most about the Church?
I struggle with the tendency of the Church to suck me out of the world, rather than send me out into it.

173] Malcolm Egner, Dalit Freedom Network, www.dfn.org.uk

MINISTRY FROM THE MARGINS

As we seek to embody the radical love of Jesus, to truly be the body of Christ in the world, is there a challenge to us to live *with*, *among* and *alongside* those in need, to minister not to the margins but *from* the margins of society? Bryan Stone suggests not only that this challenge is there for us, but that to respond to it may even be the key to our future as a Church:

'Ironically, it may be that it is precisely from a position of marginality that the Church is best able to announce peace and to bear witness to God's peaceable reign... a Church at the periphery *of* the world may yet be a Church *for* the world.' [174]

Political activist and worship leader Andy Flannagan finds the roots of just such a call in the ancient prophets of Israel. Inspired by the words of Amos 5:23-24, he wonders how God might feel when our churches 'worship' without truly embodying love or engaging with the needs of our world:

'I hate your festivals. I cannot stand your worship events. Even though there are thousands of people, and the PA could cause an earthquake, I will not accept them. Even though the band is fantastic, and you have the best worship leader in the world, I have no regard for them. Do you think I care who sells most CDs? Do you think I care what the cool new song is? Away with this individualised, feel-good soundtrack of iPod 'worship'. I'm listening to another channel. It's called Justice and Righteousness, and its arriving on a broadband connection that is wider than you can ever imagine. That's what I want to hear. I know when someone's playing my song.' [175]

Workout
Move to the Margins

What might a move 'to the margins' mean for your community of faith? How might worship, teaching, children's and youth ministry and the church's outreach programmes reflect such a move? What would be the effects - positive and negative - of such a change in our Churches?

Here, then is our challenge: to move beyond talking and singing *about* God's love to truly embodying it; to move beyond talking *to* the poor to learn to walk *with* the poor; to incarnate, in all we do, the *shalom* peace of the reign of God. Only by embracing these challenges will we join God in transforming the world. Only by hearing the call to incarnate love will we truly live out our call to be *the body of Christ*.

Speaker's Corner
The Best and Worst of the Church
Bishop Graham Cray

What do you love most about the Church?
What I love most about the Church is community and its capacity for mission.

What do you struggle with most about the Church?
What I struggle with most is its capacity to be introverted and forget its missionary call.

174] Bryan P Stone, *Evangelism After Christendom: The Theology and Practice of Christian Witness*, Brazos Press, 2006
175] Andy Flannagan, *Spring Harvest Praise 08/09*

TAKE SPRING HARVEST HOME... TAKEAWAYS FROM HOPE

The Olympic rowing team at the last Olympics had one over-riding statement they kept using, when deciding whether they should go to the opening ceremony, go for a meal, or whatever, and that was 'by doing that does it make our boat go faster?' I find this to be a fascinating statement in relation to focus, vision, drive and energy.

The HOPE story came from a similar point of view ... that as the Church works together the job is done quicker in communicating the gospel with both *words* and *deeds*. The goal of HOPE is churches doing more, together in mission, in words and deeds. One of the challenges is to place the local church at the centre of transformation within a community. It is exciting when that happens and people find faith as a result.

The material being presented in this session is all about how we can show love in deliberate and intentional service with random acts of kindness, putting our faith into action. As we think about the HOPE Takeaway story, what can you do? We recognise that serving needs within our communities is not us doing our own thing. Here are three ideas that you could do with others:

1 **Identify** with a particular need in your community. Ask people within your church whether they are aware of a particular need with which the Church could engage, which could be either multi-generational or one particular group within society. Many HOPE initiatives have started very small. One such project was in Lancaster, when the churches linked up with a project that was already happening, called Street Pride. As a result of that one project when the Church served them, two people who had been thinking about joining a church took that step. Word and actions are two sides of the same coin in relation to the gospel.

2 **Pray** as a group of churches: take time to pray together and ask for hearts to be changed, and ask God to move within your community. Most HOPE initiatives that are born out through the community are as a result of people praying together. Don't underestimate the power of relationships being built when people pray together.

3 HOPE came about over this last decade through events like Festival Manchester, Soul In the City, and Ignite Cardiff - because young people had embraced the fact that the gospel must result in community transformation. As we seek to serve in these communities we tell the story of why and what we do, showing our hearts have been changed.

Laurence Singlehurst and Roy Crowne, HOPE
www.hopetogether.org.uk

PRAYER LEADS TO ACTION

Debra Green

Following on from seven years of city-wide inter-denominational, concerted, united, and outwardly focused prayer, the churches in Greater Manchester held a large-scale festival in the city encouraging churches to reach out to the community with social action. In 2003 I was part of a team working on Festival Manchester, where over 500 churches reached out to local communities with practical acts of kindness and social action projects. Following the festival other cities began to ask for advice about city transformation principals and this led to a call from God for me to start a charity. 'Redeeming Our Communities' (ROC) was founded in 2004. ROC has multi-agency-working at the centre of all we do and it has proved to be a successful model. We bring together community groups, churches, the police, the fire service, local authorities and voluntary agencies to encourage them to work together in positive partnerships for practical change. As a result, statutory agencies have improved access to the support of Christians and church groups, and thousands of volunteers are enabled to better serve the needs of their community. This idea is proving to be even more valuable in the light of the current economic climate and the challenge of the Big Society.

Why use the word redeem?

Wikipedia defines the word 'Redeem' in several ways '...to free someone from pain or a bad situation; to restore the honour, worth, or reputation of; and to set free; rescue or ransom. In the Church we usually think in terms of redeeming a human life, which is real and wonderful. But God is also concerned for the whole of his creation; for both people and places. A city can be fallen or it can reflect his glory. Jesus speaks tenderly over Jerusalem in Matthew 23:37 'How often I have longed to gather your children together, as a hen gathers her chicks under her wings, but you were not willing'. John Greenleaf says 'the problem with society is that no one loves the institutions, we fear and dislike the structures, we are overawed and repelled by them, we submit to them and are seduced and bought by them. But we do not care for them (care is love in action).'

Tom Marshall in his book *Understanding Leadership* devotes a whole chapter, 'Cities Revisited', to how God views a city. He says 'There is evidence to show that social transformation whether it is in a culture, city or in the life of an organisation, is usually accomplished by a movement which has the specific aim of bringing about the changes necessary. Successful movements are always conceptually radical and based on religious commitment. He goes on to say: 'A movement does not require a majority in favour before it can be launched but it does need agreement amongst those who are on board.'

ROC, as a movement for change, is now seven years old and we are overwhelmed by the growing momentum across the nation. Many volunteers have caught the vision and become ROC Ambassadors, starting projects and town-wide ROC initiatives. We have seen many new community projects emerge like the ROC Café, a multi-agency youth club, which has a proven track record in reducing crime. Young people love the ROC Café; one young boy from a home where his mum has to work all hours to make ends meet described it as 'the living room I don't have at home'. The police also love the ROC Cafés, reporting between 25% and 55% reduction in anti-social behaviour where the Cafés are located. A new ROC Café project recently opened in Cobridge, Stoke, and is proving to be a great success after only a few weeks. This model can work anywhere in the UK and we would love to hear from any churches interested in partnering with us.

www.roc.uk.com

So What?
ROC

At the heart of the journey of 'Redeeming Our Communities', are principles of Church unity, prayer and networking with statutory and voluntary agencies. What scope do you see for such principles to grow in your area? Are there prayer initiatives that might lead in this direction? How easy do the churches find it to work in partnership? How aware are church members of the needs of their area and the issues facing their city or community? If God called you to take a lead in this area, what would your first steps be?

Speaker's Corner
The Best and Worst of the Church
Kate Coleman

What do you love most about the Church?
People

What do you struggle with most about the Church?
People

CELEBRATE GOD'S BRILLIANT IDEA

This session has explored what it means to be the Body of Christ: continuing to touch the world in love just as Jesus himself did. We have spoken of the transformation God is bringing to the world through a revolution of servant love, and the part we have to play in it. We have been reminded that there is good news for the poor in the coming of God's kingdom, and that it is *through his people* that God seeks to love the world. What can we celebrate in this brilliant idea?

1. We can celebrate the fact that God has come in the flesh, to touch and heal us. Christ has made the love of God visible to us. He has embodied God's passion for us.

2. We can rejoice at the thousands of ways in which the Church, Christ's body, touches and blesses those in need across the world today: the acts of compassion that bring relief and blessing to millions. We can thank God for every cup of water delivered in the name of Christ.

3. We can celebrate the incredible hope that the compassion and mercy of Christ offer us; that change is possible; that the most blighted and distorted life can be redeemed.

4. We can thank God for the waves of compassionate action that are sweeping through his Church in our age, as the people of God hear his call to love and bless the poor.

5. Above all this, we can rejoice in God's determination to transform the world. We can join the Apostle John in embracing the dream of God:

I heard a loud shout from the throne, saying, 'Look, God's home is now among his people! He will live with them, and they will be his people. God himself will be with them. He will wipe every tear from their eyes, and there will be no more death or sorrow or crying or pain. All these things are gone forever.' And the one sitting on the throne said, 'Look, I am making everything new! [176]

176] Revelation 21:3-5 *New Living Translation (NLT)*

NOTES

4
make
them
one

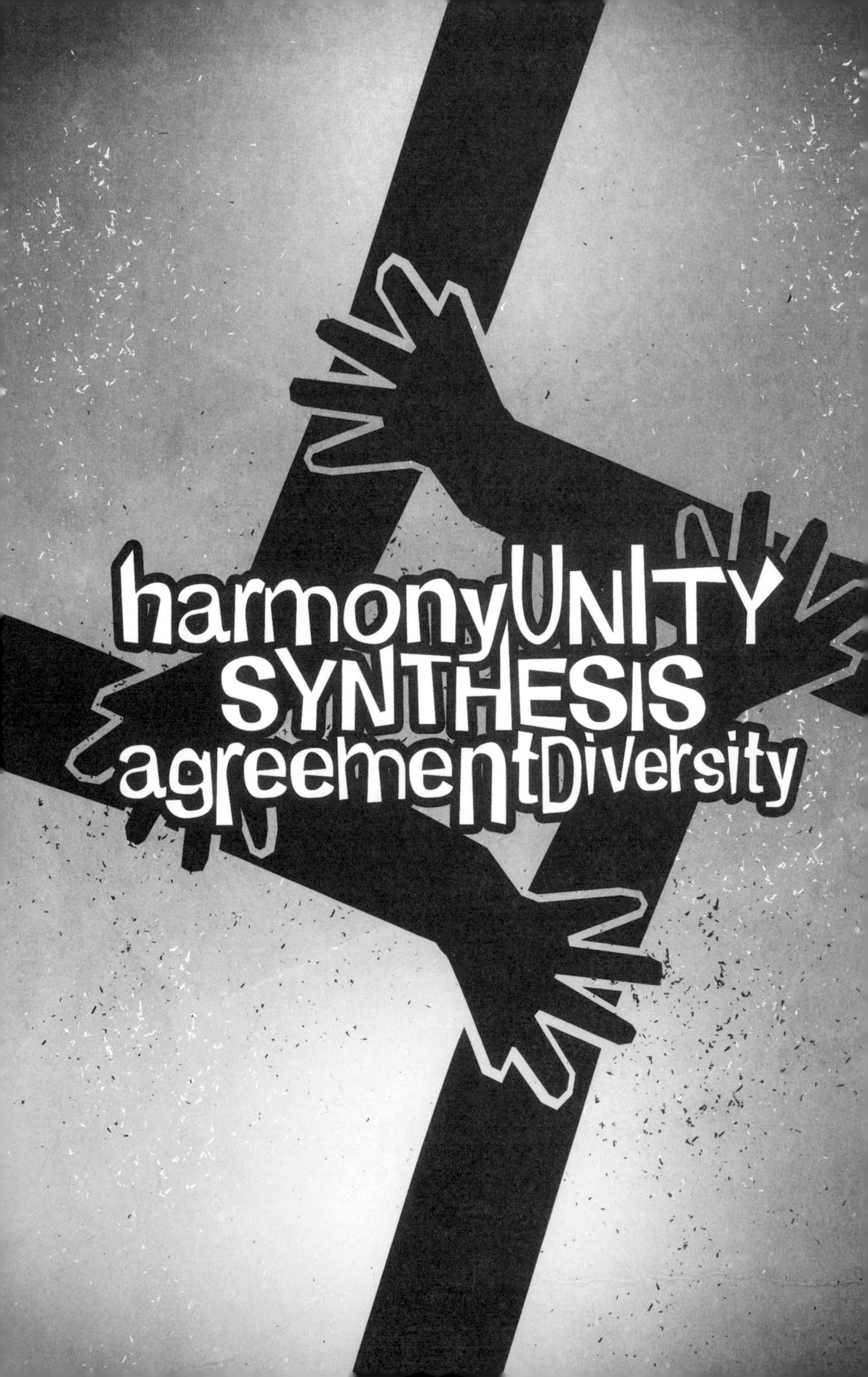
harmonyUNITY
SYNTHESIS
agreementDiversity

make them one

THE CHURCH AS THE BRIDE OF CHRIST

WHAT WILL WE DISCOVER IN THIS *CHURCH ACTUALLY* SESSION?

» That the Church cannot ever belong to any one culture, but is God's gift to the world, inviting the whole human family into united joy.

» That the future we are moving towards is an act of united worship, in which many languages will honour the one Lamb when all the tribes are gathered around one throne.

» That there is joy, now, in celebrating the diversity God has given us, and in anticipating the global unity he has paid for and will bring.

» That the Church is called not just to deliver Christ's message *to* every culture, but to listen to and learn *from* every culture, letting the many colours of God's family shape our understanding and practice.

» That God speaks every language and will gladly translate his story into every human culture and context, moving into every neighbourhood that welcomes him.

» That participation in God's global, multi-ethnic plan requires us to reach out to the 'other', overcoming fear and prejudice to know and love those unlike us; embodying embrace, not exclusion, as the mark of the gospel.

The brilliance of God's Church comes, in part, from the many colours it contains. Like a diamond it shines with a thousand different lights. Why? Because, in the Church, God has chosen to bring together all the diversity of the human family: every size and shape, every character and condition, every colour and culture.

God is preparing a bride for his son, [177] reflecting the radiant beauty of the human race. And that beauty comes, in part, from diversity. The more, different people you bring together the more amazed you are at God's artistry. God has not created a dull species, ugly in uniformity and shallow in sameness. He has made a collage. A kaleidoscope. A carnival of colour. More than any other aspect of the created world, the human family bears the image of God. And God is beautiful.

Like a jigsaw of infinite variety and scope, the picture of God grows bigger as more people are added to it. The Church is his self-portrait, intended to show us just how wide and long and high and deep his love is. Wide enough for you to be included. Long enough for me. High enough for all my friends. Deep enough for my every enemy. Through the Church, God wants us to get the full picture. He has something he wants to shjjow the angels. And we're it.

177] John 3:29, 2 Corinthians 11:2, Revelation 19:7, 21:2, 21:9, 22:17

GOD OF ALL CULTURES

Japanese theologian Kosuke Koyama, who died in 2009 aged 79, was one of the 20th Century's leading voices in bridging Western with non-Western theologies. He worked consistently to develop dialogue between European and American institutions of academic theology and the cultures of South East Asia, particularly of Thailand and Japan. He believed that the Christian gospel addressed every human culture in both affirmation and challenge. Contextualisation, he writes, is a two-stage process:

'First, to articulate Jesus Christ in culturally appropriate, communicatively apt words; and second, to criticize, reform, dethrone, or oppose culture if it is found to be against what the name of Jesus Christ stands for.' [178]

Japanese by nationality, Western by theological training, and serving as a missionary in rural Thailand, Koyama insisted that the God of Jesus Christ is the God of all cultures. He dates his discovery of this vital truth to the moment of his own conversion. At the age of 15, at the height of World War II, he experienced the horrors of the American Air Force carpet-bombing his homeland.

He writes:

'In the morning ... I saw the sun rise as usual. As though nothing had happened in the human world. The light and warmth of the sun embraced both the dead and the living. The sun quietly erased the distinction between enemy and friend. I became aware that a strange quietness had descended on me. I heard, or felt, the words of Jesus, that God 'makes his sun to rise on the evil and the good, and sends rain on the righteous and the unrighteous'. These words have come back to me from time to time for nearly 60 years since that morning. When I was baptised during the war, the minister told me that God loves everyone, Americans as well as Japanese. I was baptised, not into the religion of the enemy country, but into the God of all nations.' [179]

Koyama's conviction that he had met with a truly global God enabled him not only to study theology in America, but to apply his learning to the lives of the simple Buddhist peasants amongst whom he served as a missionary to Thailand. As a teacher of theology in Thailand, Singapore, New Zealand and America, he continued to explore the nature of faith as a gift to all cultures, and of Jesus as the 'God of all nations'.

178] Kosuke Koyama, *Water Buffalo Theology (25th Anniversary Edition, Revised and Expanded)*, Orbis, 199, Preface
179] Kosuke Koyama, Currents in Theology and Mission, April 2003, cited in David W Smith, *Against the Stream, Christianity and Mission in an Age of Globalisation*, IVP, 2003

Workout
Completing the Picture

Take a moment to reflect on the ethnic mix of the city or community in which you live. How many distinct cultures or language groups are represented there? Now repeat the exercise for your Church? Compare the two lists: who from the first is missing from the second? What can you do to change this?

JEWISH BIBLE: GLOBAL FAITH

This global faith is derived from the scriptures of the Old and New Testaments but is spoken into cultures and people groups who make no appearance in these same scriptures. At the time of the New Testament, no contact had ever been made between Jewish or Christian cultures and those of Japan, Thailand or Singapore. America and New Zealand, for their part, did not even exist in the form they do today. And yet Koyama was able to assert that the Bible's God was also God in all these places, and that the Bible's stories could speak here too. That this is possible is due to a distinctive element in New Testament theology and in the picture of the Church presented in it. In its eschatological vision of the people of God, looking to the far-future, the New Testament anticipates and proclaims a truly global faith. The followers of Jesus of Nazareth will be drawn from every culture, people-group and language on the face of the earth. Central to this future vision is the image of God's people as the Bride of Christ.

HERE COMES THE BRIDE

The use of the term 'Bride of Christ' to describe the Church has three sources in the New Testament.

» In the Gospels, Jesus uses a number of parables with this image at their heart. He is the bridegroom and his followers the bride, and a great banquet is spoken of, when their union will be celebrated. [180]

» In the Epistles this same metaphor is used again, describing the relationship of Christ with the Church as that of a husband and wife. Paul goes even further than this in his letter to the Ephesians, suggesting that human marriage is itself an image or reflection of the relationship between Christ and the Church. [181]

» In the book of Revelation, the Apostle John speaks explicitly of the Church as the Bride of Christ and uses the language of splendour and magnificence to describe her beauty. [182]

The references to the Bride of Christ in John's vision confirm that the most significant aspect of this image is its future-focus: it is an eschatological image. On the surface, the bridal language of the Gospels and Epistles describes an actual, existent relationship between Jesus and the Church - but even these passages also look forward, hinting at the joy that is to come when this marriage is finally made real and celebrated in a great feast. [183] In John's Revelation the hint becomes a shout, as John looks forward to the moment when Christ is united with his splendid and beautiful bride: a Church radiant and pure and ready to meet Christ. In the course of his vision, described as 'the wedding supper of the Lamb,' [184] John notes something very particular about this radiant Church: it is drawn from 'every nation, tribe, people and language'. [185]

The image of the Bride of Christ is a measure of overwhelming love of God for human beings. God loves each of us, and all of us, with a love beyond imagination. By the time you close the last pages of the New Testament you are left in no doubt: God is drawing together a truly global family. All the colours of humanity will be present in God's bride. To proclaim the Church as the Bride of Christ is to anticipate this future: to celebrate now the beauty and joy God is so looking forward to.

180] See Matthew 9:14-16, Mark 2:18-21, Luke 5:33-35, Matthew 22:1-13, Matthew 25:1-11,
181] Ephesians 4:32
182] Revelation 19:7, 21:2, 21:9, 22:17
183] See for example Matthew 22:1, Matthew 25:1, Ephesians 4:27
184] Revelation 19:7
185] Revelation 7:9

Workout
Here Comes the Bride

The previous paragraph suggests that the Church should reflect cultural diversity now because that is the future it is heading towards. Does this assertion make sense to you? How far is your present church from the picture of multi-cultural, multi-lingual worship of Revelation 7:9? What actions or activities might begin to change this?

MANY LANGUAGES, ONE LAMB

In his lifetime John saw the Church spread through Asia Minor and into the fringes of Europe. He saw the message accepted first by Jews, then by 'God-fearing Gentiles' - foreigners already attracted to Jewish beliefs - and finally by pagans, complete outsiders to the Jewish world. But his experience is far from global. His own travels were contained within a tightly defined region of Asia Minor. He witnessed the power of love to overcome difference and bring former enemies into reconciled relationship, but he knew much of the world was yet to be included. However his vision of the heavenly future is explicitly global in scope and remarkable for its boldness and its breadth: *Every* tribe and language is included. There will be one family. One body. One Bride of Christ - beautiful precisely because she is so colourful. When the focus of the vision shifts and it is a city that John sees, radiant with the splendour of God, he still understands that it will be home to 'the nations of the world'. The splendour of kings will be brought into this city [186] - the glory and honour of the nations. [187] Despite the limitations of his own experience, John knows that the gospel will go global, and that God is calling to himself *one* people drawn from the world's *many* peoples.

The global family John foresees is a single united people rich with the colour and diversity of humanity and alive with the many languages humans speak. They praise in many different languages, but all their praise is offered to the one Lamb. This is the Bride of Christ: thousands of different people-groups, made one in Christ. The movement that began in Jerusalem on the Day of Pentecost will go on until it has touched every nation on earth: and in every place it touches, the Church will emerge, as diverse peoples are drawn into the one, new family God is forming. The apostle who remembers the promise of Jesus to 'draw all people' to himself [188] is the same apostle who dreams here of what that great global gathering will look like. John's vision of the Bride of Christ suggests that the *forming of the Church* is central to the purposes of God in history, and that *cultural and ethnic diversity* is central to the forming of the Church. The Church, Wolfhart Pannenberg writes

'...is the eschatological people of God gathered out of all peoples, and it is thus a sign of reconciliation for a future unity of a renewed humanity in the kingdom of God.' [189]

To embrace Christ is to embrace his desire for one global family. To declare myself a Christian is to step into the most ethnically and culturally diverse movement in history. To name the Church the *Bride of Christ* is to look forward with expectation and joy to a future in which I will stand with the peoples of every tribe and language and, with them, worship the one Lamb. To worship *now* is to anticipate that future. This offers three key challenges to our churches. Accepting our identity as the Bride of Christ will mean:

Experiencing here and now the joy of our diversity.
For the New Testament Church, *where we're going is part of who we are*. If we are destined to become a multi-coloured, multi-lingual worshipping community, then that's what we will celebrate being now. Diversity adds to our understanding of God. Every colour incorporated into worship increases the richness of our picture of God.

Embracing the call of God to reach every tribe and culture.
If the end-game of the Church is worship involving every tribe and tongue, then co-operating with the

186] Revelation 21:25
187] Revelation 21:26
188] John 12:32
189] Wolfhart Pannenberg, *Cited* in Veli-Matti Kärkkäinen *An Introduction to Ecclesiology: Ecumenical, Historical and Global Perspectives*, IVP, 2002

Spirit *now* will involve expressing the gospel in every language and culture. Translating the 'unsearchable riches of Christ' into every cultural and tribal setting is the present-day task and joy of the Church.

Escaping cultural captivity to express love for the 'other'.

For each one of us the journey towards the wedding feast of the Lamb will involve meeting, knowing and coming to love many people from cultures other than our own. Learning to embrace rather than exclude those unlike us, is a vital part of the journey of God's Church.

THE JOY OF OUR DIVERSITY

GOD HAS MADE US DIFFERENT AND CALLS US TO ENJOY THE MANY COLOURS HE HAS GIVEN

Martin Luther King Jr once famously described eleven o'clock on a Sunday morning as *'the most segregated hour in Christian America'*. Far from celebrating the joys of diversity, many of the churches of his day reinforced social divisions. This couldn't be further from the vision presented in the New Testament. Graham Tomlin comments:

'The Church of Jesus Christ has therefore become for Paul the place where the promised reconciliation takes place. It is the place where everything that wants to be is brought together under Christ. A broken and divided creation is finally reconciled to itself and to God in the Body of Christ. In the light of all this, perhaps it begins to dawn on us why Paul gets so excited about the idea of Gentiles coming to Church, sitting next to Jews, and handing them the communion cup. Here is the 'hard evidence' of his grand exhilarating vision.' [190]

Unity in diversity was not only the eschatological hope of the New Testament Church, it was a lived reality. Public worship, for these congregations, anticipated the great feast God has promised. The joys of the unity

that was to come were celebrated in the unity that had already arrived.

For many contemporary observers, this is a vital and indispensable aspect of God's mission. Chad Brennan is an American church leader who has pioneered the concept of multi-ethnic churches, calling the vision of an many-coloured church 'the new culture'. He is openly critical of the ways churches and missions have ignored the call to 'togetherness' to pursue mono-cultural models of ministry. He writes:

'I can vividly remember a conversation I had several years ago with a friend who was a national director of a large ministry. We were talking about their organisation and how they planned to address the increasing amount of ethnic diversity in the locations where they were active. He explained how they were creating separate ministries for each ethnic group in those locations in order to 'most effectively reach them with the gospel' because 'most people want to be with their own ethnicity'. When I asked if they had plans to eventually try to bring the different ethnic groups together into a multi-ethnic group he explained that they did not because it would 'create an extra barrier to the gospel' and then stated emphatically, 'There is no biblical mandate for bringing people together of different ethnicities.' Do you believe that is true? How would you respond?' [191]

190] Graham Tomlin, *The Provocative Church*, SPCK, 2002 and 2004, p163
191] Chad Brennan, 7 Principles of the New Culture, http://thenewculture.org/articles/principles-1-cb/

Workout
Visible Reconciliation

What does reconciliation look like? In a room filled with people of different cultures and races, how would you know who was reconciled and who was not? What signs would you look for? How might our programmes, activities and actions as the Church reflect these signs? Are there opportunities in your gatherings for people of different backgrounds to make visible their reconciliation in Christ?

FROM MULTICULTURAL TO INTERCULTURAL

Brennan is among a growing number of church leaders who believe that the Church is specifically called to celebrate cultural diversity and to express visibly the coming together of cultural groups in reconciled relationship. This also reflects some of the most recent thinking in inter-cultural dialogue, where practitioners are urging a move beyond 'multicultural' to an 'intercultural' processes. The key difference is that where multiculturalism can easily become little more than tolerance, an intercultural approach will be active in seeking dialogue. The 2004 report *Planning for the Intercultural City* suggests that:

'The intercultural approach goes beyond equal opportunities and respect for existing cultural differences to the pluralist transformation of public space, institutions and civic culture. It does not recognise cultural boundaries as fixed but in a state of flux and remaking. An intercultural approach aims to facilitate dialogue, exchange and reciprocal understanding between people of different backgrounds.' [192]

Workout
Metacultural Church

*The description above of an intercultural rather than multicultural approach has implications for the Church. It suggests a setting in which a Church not only **attracts** people from diverse cultural backgrounds, but seeks **input** and **involvement** from those many cultures. What might the implications of this be in your setting for:*

» The language styles and vocabulary used in services and prayers?

» The musical styles of worship?

» The pattern or cycle of worship services?

Is it possible for the Church to be a genuinely intercultural experience?

192] J Bloomfield and F Bianchini, *Planning for the Intercultural City*, Comedia, 2004 cited in Phil Wood, Charles Landry and Jude Bloomfield, *Cultural Diversity in Britain: A Toolkit for Cross-cultural Co-operation*, Comedia / The Joseph Rowntree Foundation, 2006

FROM GLOBAL TO METANATIONAL

In the business world, a similar argument has led to the shift from speaking of 'multinational' corporations to describing those that are 'metanational'. These are companies that not only operate in several countries and cultures, but are also able to make use of the insights, assets and input drawn from those different cultures. They are not merely an assembly of different ethnic groups but are shaped by interaction amongst those groups. Metanational companies succeed...

'By discovering, accessing, mobilizing, and leveraging knowledge from many locations around the world'. [193]

The concept of an *intercultural* or *metanational* community is much closer to the biblical picture of the Church than simple multi-culturalism. In the Church, different groups do not only tolerate one another - they learn from one another. They benefit from difference and grow through being together. Thus the Apostle Paul is able to point repeatedly, as evidence of the workings of God's grace, to the fact that in the Church men and women, Jews and Gentiles, slaves and slave owners and educated and uneducated people are brought together in mutual submission to learn, love and grow. For Paul, the one-time Pharisee taught from infancy to fear and despise Gentile culture, this is a core expression of the work of Christ. Colin Sinclair in his notes on Philippians, sees this in the foundations of this particular church, built on the conversion of a successful business woman, [194] a trafficked slave girl [195] and a prominent Gentile civil servant: [196]

'The story of the beginning of this church is told graphically in Acts 16. The three conversions related there have added humour when you remember that Paul, when still Paul the Pharisee, would have prayed daily 'Lord, I thank you that I am not a slave, a woman or a Gentile' - for these three groupings made up the Philippian church!' [197]

Here is a church with only three members that is already a celebration of diversity, and for Paul an experience of 'culture-crossing' at multiple levels. At its heart is the experience of grace, and the working out of that grace in reconciled relationships. It is not without significance that years later Paul was still encouraging the members of this same church to live in holy reconciliation. [198] Apartheid [199] was not an option. There would be one community; one family into which all were grafted. Christ is returning for one bride.

193] Yves L Doz, Jose Santos and Peter Williamson, *Global to Metanational, How Companies Win in the Knowledge Economy*, Harvard Business Press, 2001 see http://hbswk.hbs.edu/archive/2679.html
194] Acts 16:13-15
195] Acts 16:15-18
196] Acts 16:25-34
197] Colin Sinclair, *The Hitch-Hiker's Guide to the Bible: Thumbing through the Old and New Testaments,* Monarch, 2008
198] Philippians 4:2
199] Literally 'separate development'

So What?
Metanational

Many UK churches do not have, in terms of race, a multi-ethnic membership. Some are mono-cultural in their congregational make-up, and don't see many opportunities to change this. How can such churches celebrate the global diversity of the Bride of Christ? Two strategies that many local churches have found helpful are:

Local Links. *Are there other churches and congregations in your area whose ethnic make-up is different to your own? What can you do to forge links with them? Are there joint projects you can work on together? Is united worship - even from time to time - possible?*

Global Give and Take. *How can you express solidarity and partnership with the world Church? Are there twinning or exchange arrangements you can invest in? How can you make sure that these are opportunities not only to give but to receive: genuine expressions of mutual listening and learning?*

CULTURAL DIVERSITY: BIBLICAL UNITY

The Church is to be a foretaste and a sign of God's intentions for the wider human family. Timothy Keller writes:

'Because creation was made in the image of God who is equally one and many, the human race will finally be reunited and yet our racial and cultural diversity will remain intact in the renewed world. The human race finally lives together in peace and interdependence. *Glory to God in the highest* goes with *peace on earth*.'[200]

The vision of unity in diversity touches on all the 'natural' or cultural distinctions applied to human societies, but some of the key distinctions mentioned in the New Testament and relevant for the Church today are:

» **Race:** there are consistent New Testament references to the uniting of races

» **Language:** in that it represents difference and also helps or hinders relationship

» **Education:** in the sense that 'cultured' and 'uncultured' people worship together

» **Gender:** male and female reconciliation is a recurring New Testament theme

---

200] Timothy Keller, *The Reason for God: Belief in an Age of Scepticism,* Hodder and Stoughton, 2008

» **Age:** parent-child relationships and care for the elderly, are explicitly mentioned

» **Economics:** slaves and slave-owners are the extremes of economic difference

» **Conflict:** those who have been enemies are explicitly named as reconciled

It is significant that in many of our churches several of these distinctions are the very lines along which we draw ministry boundaries. Jim Belcher, in *Deep Church* recounts his own disillusionment with 'fragmented' ministry plans:

'...we discovered that life-stage ministry segregates the Church. Add to this the creation of worship services with a musical style targeted to a particular age group and the Church is no longer what it is supposed to be - a family with all ages worshiping together...We decided that age segregation impoverished both individuals and the community.' [201]

Workout
Signs of Difference

Consider the list of cultural distinctives. How many of these differences are present in your community of faith? Where they are, what do you do to celebrate diversity and express unity? What more could you do?

ONE PEOPLE: ONE TABLE

The event that most embodies the Church's eschatological hope, in which we look forward to coming day of 'many languages: one Lamb', is the Eucharistic meal, the Lord's supper. This is the central sacrament around which the global Church gathers, the banquet of God from which no human culture is excluded. Here human beings of every shape and stripe come together. Here all are equal - even the betrayer may sit alongside the betrayed. Here we come on the basis, not of the talents or qualifications of achievements we bring but of the righteousness of Christ. The Eucharist is the 'one table' that makes of the global Church one body.

Workout
Broken Body

How does your regular celebration of the Eucharist / Lord's Supper celebrate the 'one body' into which Christ has brought his followers? What could you do in this aspect of your worship to show your appreciation of:

» *The diversity found in your church*
» *The diversity of the wider city or community in which you live*
» *The richness of God's global family*

201] Jim Belcher, *Deep Church: A Third Way Beyond Emerging and Traditional*, IVP, 2009

MORE THREADS: MORE BEAUTY

In its public worship, but also in its mission activity, its social expression and its sense of community, the Church offers a sign of God's promised unity: a visual aid for the trajectory of the gospel. Steve Chalke and Anthony Watkis write:

'The Church modeling diversity in harmony serves as a prophetic sign to our society. As it finds ways of creating, building and connecting truly diverse communities rather than mirroring a society divided by race, creed, age, income, gender and the rest, it announces the kingdom of God is here.... The greater the number of threads in the tapestry of any local church, the more attractive and effective it becomes.' [202]

This is no sentimental vision of the world drinking the same cola and singing the same pop song. It is unity worked out in the hard graft of reality and relationship. Differences are not ignored in this diverse community: they are overcome. Lis Goddard writes of the New Testament vision:

The new Christian community was to be and, from our reading of the New Testament, was (though with teething problems) a place where God was doing something new and radical. It was a place where the kingdom of God was breaking in and the new creation order was being established. The early Church didn't always get it right, but it wasn't good enough for them to continue owning their brothers and sisters as slaves, insisting that their Gentile brothers should be circumcised or excluding their female members from full participation in the body of Christ. We would not expect to return to that way of living today, we we recognise that it is in no way consonant with the gospel. [203]

Rose Dowsett has also pointed out that this unity is hard-won. The celebration of diversity will not come without the relinquishing of privilege. But the Bible is clear: all believers are equal in Christ:

'That great plank of the Reformation, the priesthood of all believers, sometimes appears to be believed to mean 'the priesthood of all white Anglo-Saxon English-speaking male believers'. But, in a family where God has broken down the dividing walls of ethnicity, social status and gender, and replaced them in Christ with an equality between different members of the family as sons and daughters, we need to think again - and with great humility - about how we are going to relate to one another with love and respect.' [204]

So What?
All Believers

Rose Dowsett suggests that the 'priesthood of all believers' might be a challenge to the ways we operate as the Church. How can this ancient idea help you, in your local setting, to include everyone? What steps can you take to increase the visible engagement of people from different backgrounds?

Speaker's Corner
The Best and Worst of the Church
Fran Beckett

What do you love most about the Church?
The opportunity for and experience of a motley bunch of people being community, with God at the centre – a safe yet challenging place in which to explore what loving God and loving our neighbour is all about.

What do you struggle with most about the Church?
When we reduce it to a consumer experience, with 'me' at the centre, and when what we focus on in our time together bears little relevance to our everyday lives.

202] Steve Chalke and Anthony Watkis, *Intelligent Church: A Journey Towards Christ-Centred Community,* Zondervan, 2006
203] Lis Goddard in Lis Goddard and Clare Hendry, *The Gender Agenda: Discovering God's Plan for Church Leadership,* IVP, 2010
204] Rose Dowsett, 'Rainbow Theology: Grace in Diversity' cited in Jeff Lucas, *One People: Celebrating the One True God,* Spring Harvest, 2007

EVERY TRIBE AND CULTURE

GOD'S STORY CAN BE TOLD IN EVERY LANGUAGE AND HAS A HOME IN EVERY HUMAN CULTURE

In his exploration of Christian mission, Stephen Gaukroger paints a compelling picture of the purpose and goal of missional activity.

'The Bible has a captivating view of the goal or climax of mission. It describes a future in which every language, people group and country will be represented altogether in a magnificent display of international co-operation and harmony (Revelation 7:9). The whole of history is moving towards this stupendous conclusion: a planet-wide worship and celebration event drawn from all the nations of the globe under the Lordship of Jesus.' [205]

The diversity that has implications for the unity of our worship and ministry also has implications for the breadth of our understanding of mission. Does the life and practice of our local congregations truly reflect God's desire to form for himself one planet-wide family?

GOD THE POLYGLOT

A polyglot is someone who knows or uses several languages. Wikipedia lists the world's greatest polyglots as:

» **Uku Masing** (1909–1985), an Estonian linguist, theologian, ethnologist, and poet, who claimed fluency in approximately 65 languages and translated from 20.

» **Harold Williams** (1876–1928), a New Zealand journalist and linguist who claimed to speak over 58 languages.

» **Ziad Fazah** (1954–), who was raised in Lebanon, has lived in Brazil since the 1970s and claims to speak, read and understand 58 languages.

» **William James Sidis** (1898–1944) an American child prodigy who at the year of his death could speak over 40 languages. He was able to learn one language per week.

» **Giuseppe Mezzofanti** (1774-1849) an Italian Cardinal who spoke 39 languages fluently.

The assertion of Christian mission is that these talents pale into insignificance before God, whose story can be told in every human language. Timothy Tennet, who refers to Christianity as 'the largest, most ethnically diverse religion in the world', credits this to the 'theological translatability' of the faith. He writes that:

The lifeblood of Christianity is found in its ability to translate itself across new cultural and geographic barriers and to recognise that eras that were once the mission field can, over time, become the very heart of Christian vitality... [206]

God is the ultimate polyglot, speaking every language known and inviting every human being to pray in their own mother tongue. How can a Church resulting from the love of such a God *not* be globally diverse?

205] Stephen Gaukroger, *Why Bother With Mission?* IVP, 1996
206] Timothy C Tennent, *Theology in the Context of World Christianity*, Zondervan, 2007

To worship a polyglot God is to embrace his desire for diversity in worship; to join with him in reaching every tribe and tongue and to discover the cultural and theological riches that emerge when people-groups collide. Missiologist Andrew Walls suggests that it is at the 'cultural boundaries' that the richest truths emerge.

'When the gospel crosses a cultural frontier or when Christians encounter those alternative formulations of spiritual reality we call the other world faiths or religions, new situations arise that require Christians to make a Christian choice and to formulate the reasons for that choice... The greatest religious fact of our time is the deepening Christian engagement with the cultures and religions of Africa, Asia and Latin America.'[207]

Workout
Mission Boundaries

Andrew Walls suggests that it is at the boundaries of mission that innovation and renewal take place. His examples are of the encounter of the Christian story with African, Asian and Latin American cultures. What are the equivalent boundaries in your local situation? Where do you see the encounter with those outside your faith community adding richness and newness to your faith? Where would you turn to if you were looking for this experience?

HOME AND AWAY

Embracing diversity in mission used to mean travelling. It no longer does. The cities of Europe have become, in themselves, melting-pots of diversity. London leads the way:

'London is now more diverse than any city that has ever existed. Altogether, more than 300 languages are spoken by the people of London, and the city has at least 50 non-indigenous communities with populations of 10,000 or more. Virtually every race, nation, culture and religion in the world can claim at least a handful of Londoners.' [208]

Other UK cities are not far behind:

'While London represents a unique kind of diversity, the rest of Britain is now changing. In 1997, a total of 63,000 work-permit holders and their dependents came to Britain. In 2003, it was 119,000. Altogether, between 1991 and 2001, the UK population increased by 2.2 million, some 1.14 million of whom were born abroad. And all this was before EU enlargement in May 2004, which brought 130,000 more people from the new member states in its first year alone.

There are 37,000 Pakistan-born people in Birmingham and 27,500 in Bradford, 25,000 Indians in Leicester, 4,000 Bangladeshis in Oldham and 4,000 West Indians in Nottingham. There are now over 1,000 French people living in Bristol and Brighton, 650 Greeks in Colchester, 600 Portuguese in Bournemouth and Poole, 800 Poles in Bradford, 1,300 Somalis in Sheffield, 770 Zimbabweans in Luton, 370 Iranians in Newcastle and 400 in Stockport, and 240 Malaysians in Southsea.' [209]

The figures are arresting, and even more so when we reflect that most of our theology has been forged in an age when this was not so - not to mention the writing of our worship songs and the planning of missional strategies, which for the most part reflect our mono-cultural assumptions.

Richard Sudworth recounts first-hand experiences of these changes in inner-city Birmingham:

207] Andrew Walls in Timothy C Tennent, *Theology in the Context of World Christianity*, Zondervan, 2007

208] Phil Wood, Charles Landry and Jude Bloomfield, *Cultural Diversity in Britain: A Toolkit for Cross-cultural Co-operation*, Comedia / The Joseph Rowntree Foundation, 2006

209] Phil Wood, Charles Landry and Jude Bloomfield, *Cultural diversity in Britain: A Toolkit for Cross-cultural Co-operation*, Comedia / The Joseph Rowntree Foundation, 2006

'We used to have 120 children in the Sunday school. We had to hire another building because the church hall wasn't big enough... I can remember to this day the first non-white person I got to know. She came to our school when I was about nine or ten and she'd come with her family all the way from Kenya'. This is Anne speaking. She still lives in this area, worships at the same church, helps with the same Sunday school. The Sunday school now caters for about 30 children... That same area is now approximately 70% Muslim, most originating from the Mirpur region of Pakistan. Anne's friend from Kenya would no longer be the isolated novelty that she was. Alongside the predominant Muslim community are Somali Muslims, Hindus, Sikhs, Chinese and asylum seekers from the Middle East and Africa. This is now my neighbourhood, too, and I, with Anne, enjoy the local Asian greengrocers, kebab houses, Bhangra music and sweet stores ... As I write this, the local Asian newsagents have just put up a sign in Polish, advertising foodstuffs catering to the freshest wave of language and culture mixing in our neighbourhood. [210]

Richard's reflection on mission and ministry in a multi-cultural and multi-faith setting, published as *Distinctly Welcoming*, [211] is an excellent resource for congregations wrestling with these new realities.

Workout
Mission Opportunities

Through the 19th and 20th centuries, the churches of the UK invested massive resources in overseas missions, looking to 'export' the gospel to cultures around the world. In the later years of that same period, people from many parts of the world have been brought, by circumstance or aspiration, to the UK. What are the implications for the mission of our churches? Has God brought the world to our very doorstep for a reason? If so, how do we respond? Can we apply the principles that once shaped cross-cultural mission abroad to the ways in which we engage in mission at home?

210] Richard Sudworth, *Distinctly Welcoming: Christian Presence in a Multifaith Society*, Scripture Union, 2007
211] Richard Sudworth, *Distinctly Welcoming: Christian Presence in a Multifaith Society*, Scripture Union,

HOPEquotes: Bridging Cultures

So What?
Listen to Learn

For too long the Christian encounter with other faiths and cultures has been built on the assumptions of conversionism: we reach out to others in order to win them over. This approach has its merits and has its place: but it cannot be the whole story. There must also be a sense in which we love unconditionally and listen for the sake of learning. Every cross-cultural encounter is a learning opportunity. Can we learn to listen and listen to learn?

'HOPE PROVIDES US WITH A BANNER FOR A MORE JOINED-UP APPROACH TO LOCAL MISSION. JOINING BALSALL HEATH FORUM IS MAKING A DIFFERENCE, AND THROUGH A BRIDGING CULTURES COURSE, WE GAIN UNDERSTANDING AND BUILD FRIENDSHIPS WITH PEOPLE IN OUR AREA. WE LOVE WITH CHRIST'S LOVE - UNAFFECTED BY DIFFERENCES IN CULTURE, NATIONALITY OR RELIGIOUS PERSUASION.' [212]

CHANGING WORLD: CHANGING CHURCH

At the same time the make-up of world populations and the face of the global Church have changed more in the past 100 years than in the previous 1900. Timothy Tennet notes:

'One hundred years ago it would have seemed highly unlikely that by the dawn of the 21st century there would be more evangelicals in Nepal than in Spain. One hundred years ago few would have believed that on a typical Sunday in the year 2000 only around one million Anglicans would attend church in Great Britain compared to over seventeen million Anglicans in Sunday worship in Nigeria.' [213]

Yet for many of us, theology remains a distinctly Western enterprise.

'We continue to talk about Church history in a way that puts Europe at the centre, and Church history outside the West is reserved for those preparing for the mission field or Church historians pursuing specialist studies. We continue to think that our theological reflections are normative and universally applicable to all peoples from all cultures. In short, the Western Church has not yet fully absorbed how the dramatic shifts in global

212]Roger Lynch, community outreach worker from Riverside Church, Birmingham
213]Timothy C Tennent, *Theology in the Context of World Christianity*, Zondervan, 2007

Christianity are influencing what constitutes normative Christianity ... We must learn to think bigger, listen more, and look at the Church from a wider vista.' [214]

What might it take for our theology to be informed by the many voices of the world Church, so that diversity not only shapes our view of mission, but impacts our view of God himself? Justo Gonzalez poses the challenge:

'The fact is that the gospel is making headway among the many tribes, peoples and languages - that it is indeed making more headway among them than it is among the dominant cultures of the North Atlantic. The question is not whether there will be a multi-cultural Church. Rather, the question is whether those who have become accustomed to seeing the gospel expressed only or primarily in terms of those dominant cultures will be able to participate in the life of the multi-cultural Church that already is a reality.' [215]

Workout
Selective Deafness

*Despite the massive growth in the Christian populations of the global South, and the accelerated growth of churches and leaders in these countries, the voice of the developing world **into** our theology remains muted. We still listen more to Anglo-Saxon scholars, from both sides of the Atlantic, than we do to the world Church. How can put this right? Are there ways of truly listening to the world Church? How might this effect:*
  » ***Our readings of the Bible?***
  » ***Our understanding of mission?***
  » ***Our response to social issues?***

What can we learn from those God is raising up as leaders in the world Church?

THE NEW GLOBAILTY

Do we need our theology, and with it our ecclesiology, our understanding of mission and our practice of worship, to become more intentionally global? Do we need to take account, in Ulrich Beck's term, of the new 'globality'?

'Globality means that from now on nothing which happens on our planet is only a limited local event: all inventions, victories and catastrophes affect the whole world, and we must reorient and reorganise our lives and actions, our organisations and institutions, along a 'local-global' axis.' [216]

So What?
Racial Divides

*If we acknowledge the need for a new globality in the Church, what are the steps we can take towards meeting it? Are there racial and culture divides in our own community we can work to heal? Are even our own churches still divided? What about local-global partnerships - can we commit not only to work **with** but to learn **from** the churches of Africa, Asia and Latin America?*

Unless we can respond positively to some of these challenges, and begin to take steps toward meeting them, it is unlikely that the churches of Europe, in the coming decades, will reflect the deep and many-coloured beauty of the Bride of Christ.

214] Timothy C Tennent, *Theology in the Context of World Christianity*, Zondervan, 2007
215] Justo L Gonzalez, *For the Healing of the Nations*, Orbis 1999, cited in David W Smith, *Against the Stream: Christianity and Mission in an Age of Globalisation*, IVP, 2003
216] Ulrich Beck, *What is Globalisation?*, Polity Press, 2000, cited in David Smith, *Mission After Christendom*, Darton, Longman and Todd, 2003

LOVE FOR THE 'OTHER'

THE FUTURE GOD IS DRAWING ME TOWARDS REQUIRES ME TO REACH OUT TO THOSE UNLIKE ME

Croatian theologian Miroslav Volf has argued powerfully that the embrace of 'the other' is essential to the practice of the Christian faith. His award-winning book *Exclusion and Embrace* grew out of questions raised in his own experience by the brutal wars that engulfed the Balkans after the collapse of communism. In his introduction to the book he writes:

'After I finished my lecture Professor Jürgen Moltmann stood up and asked one of his typical questions, both concrete and penetrating: *'But can you embrace a četnik?'* It was the winter of 1993. for months now the notorious Serbian fighters called 'četnik' had been sowing desolation in my native country, herding people into concentration camps, raping women, burning down churches and destroying cities. I had just argued that we ought to embrace our enemies as God has embraced us in Christ. Can I embrace a *četnik* - the ultimate other, so to speak, the evil other? What would justify the embrace? Where would I draw the strength

for it? What would it do to my identity as a human being and as a Croat?' [217]

Volf's answer on the day was honest - and reflects the dilemma we all face as believers:

'No I cannot - but as a follower of Christ I think I should be able to.'

The question led him to explore his own reactions and those of others around him, and to examine the gap between his inability to embrace 'the other' and his deep conviction that his faith called him to do so.

We may not all be caught up in the brutality of war. The 'other' we face may not be a vicious enemy. But we are all called to reach beyond the familiar and comfortable and embrace those different from us, building heart-to-heart relationships across cultural divides: and the Church, the Bride of Christ, is intended to be a place of such relationships. This sense of stepping out of my own cultural comfort to find God in the 'other' was also a central factor in the work of Kosuke Koyama. He writes:

MY 'METHODOLOGY' IN THAILAND AND EVER SINCE, HAS BEEN 'TO SEE THE FACE OF GOD IN THE FACES OF PEOPLE' [218]

217] Miroslav Volf, *Exclusion and Embrace: A Theological Exploration of Identity, Otherness, and Reconciliation*, Abingdon Press, 1996, Introduction
218] Kosuke Koyama, *Water Buffalo Theology (25th Anniversary Edition, Revised and Expanded)*, Orbis, 199, Preface

FACE OF THE FUGITIVE

For Dutch Priest Henri Nouwen the same challenge existed *within* Western European culture. Faced with the strangeness of a young generation who had rejected the Church, Nouwen believed that only an encounter built on true listening could save the Church. In *The Wounded Healer* he uses and ancient story to convey this urgent need:

'One day a young fugitive, trying to hide himself from the enemy, entered a small village. The people were kind to him and offered him a place to stay. But when the soldiers who sought the fugitive asked where he was hiding, everyone became fearful. The soldiers threatened to burn the village and kill every man in it unless the young man were handed over to them before dawn. The people went to the minister and asked him what to do. The minister, torn between handing over the boy to the enemy or having his people killed, withdrew to his room and read his Bible, hoping to find an answer before dawn. After many hours, in the early morning his eyes fell on these words:'It is better that one man dies than that the whole people be lost.'

Then the minister closed the Bible, called the soldiers and told them where the boy was hidden. And after the soldiers led the fugitive away to be killed, there was a feast in the village because the minister had saved the lives of the people. But the minister did not celebrate. Overcome with a deep sense of sadness, he remained in his room. That night an angel came to him and asked, 'What have you done?' He said: 'I handed over the fugitive to the enemy.' Then the angel said: 'But don't you know that you have handed over the Messiah?' 'How could I know?' The minister replied anxiously. Then the angel said: 'If, instead of reading your Bible, you had visited this young man just once and looked into his eyes, you would have known.'

While versions of this story are very old, it seems the most modern of tales. Like that minister, who might have recognised the Messiah if he had raised his eyes from his Bible to look into the youth's eyes, we are challenged to look into the eyes of the young men and women of today, who are running away from our cruel ways. Perhaps that will be enough to prevent us from handing them over to the enemy and enable us to lead them out of their hidden places into the middle of their people where they can redeem us from our fears.' [219]

So What?
Facing the Fugitive

Henri Nouwen's point in the story above is not that we should abandon the Bible, or stop reading it. It is that our religious practices must not be allowed to turn us away from genuine encounter with the people God loves. Can we embrace the both/and of encountering God in his word and in his world? As you read the story, who is the fugitive in your mind? Whose story have you struggled to listen to? Whose face have you not seen? Find them Look into their eyes. Listen to them. Hear their story.

219] Henri J M Nouwen, *The Wounded Healer; In our own woundedness, we can become a source of life for others*, Darton, Longman and Todd, 1994, 2008

The courage to embrace the 'other' in this way comes, Alan and Debra Hirsch suggest, from having a right view of Jesus. Jesus is Lord of all, captain of every culture. He is the one before whose name 'every knee will bow'[221] and whose Lordship 'every tongue will confess'[222] - presumably in every known human language. No matter what my culture, I can say that I belong to Jesus. But I can never say, culturally, that he belongs to me. To imprison the risen Jesus in any given culture is to entomb him again. His very resurrection denies our cultural cages.

'To get the right view of Jesus is profoundly important both for mission and discipleship, particularly when ministering to those who don't fit our cultural stereotypes. Jesus must be freed in order to relate to all people; if he isn't freed, the incarnation fails to make sense. Jesus refuses to be put into any of our boxes. He doesn't - and never will - represent one individual over another, or the majority of the population over the minority. As the Archetypal Human, the new Adam, he represents us all. And we all need to be able to identify with Jesus. That's the whole point of the incarnation: he became a human in order to fully identify with each and every one of us.'[223]

BRIDGES OF BOYSTOWN

For Andrew and Brenda Marin the answer to these questions was that the faces they had not seen; the stories they had not heard, were in the gay, lesbian, bisexual and transgender (GLBT) communities of their own American culture. Conservative in background and theology, the Marins moved to 'Boystown', Chicago's notorious gay neighbourhood, and set about building friendships. The result has been an innovative project to build bridges of understanding between churches of all types and the GLBT communities around them. Andrew writes:

'Every stereotype can be broken with a face, and every face has a story. Even leaders in both the GLBT and the Christian community tell me they know that something needs to change - but nothing is changing because we've all been conditioned to dig in and fight. So where do we go from here? The uniqueness of the Christian faith is its call to be distinct, walking in a way that sidesteps social and cultural norms. But the Christian faith calls for a specific distinction: love.

...So we're called by Christ to be different by being loving - by choosing humility over hostility, by braving the unknown rather than huddling in safe enclaves, by daring to face people who we've offended and who have offended us, and inviting them into a reconciled relationship with God and one another.' [220]

So What?
Cultural Captivity

*Is there a racial group, people group or sub-cultural you know of but have found it difficult to love? Have you decided, worse still, that Jesus shares your view? Consider now what steps you can take to escape this cultural captivity. Your journey may begin with prayer; with a smile and conversation; perhaps even with an invitation to a dinner party. What will it take for you, before you judge, to **listen**?*

220] Andrew Marin, *Love is an Orientation: Elevating the Conversation with the Gay Community*, IVP, 2009
221] Philippians 2:10
222] Philippians 2:11
223] Alan and Debra Hirsch, *Untamed: Reactivating a Missional Form of Discipleship*, Baker Books, 2010

THE CHURCH HAS LEFT THE BUILDING

One project that has recently taken many church groups out of their buildings to embrace those they might otherwise not even meet is Street Pastors. This late-night expression of unconditional love brings Christians together across racial and denominational distinctions, to love and serve their communities. Rev Les Isaacs, founder of the project, explains:

Street Pastors has become a phenomenon in the church community, among non-churched onlookers, in the offices of central and local government, and in the eyes of people on the street. Yet long before we put a uniform on people and came up with the name 'Street Pastors' I was working with Christians who had a passion to engage with people on the street at night. They had a straightforward concern for antisocial behaviour in our towns and cities and a desire to relate to those who were searching for answers.

A phone call I took in the Evangelical Alliance office really got it started for me. A journalist was on the line. He asked why our streets were becoming plagued by antisocial behaviour and alcohol related problems. 'What is the solution?' he asked, with urgency in his voice. 'What is the Church's view on drugs, drink and gangs in the urban context?' he went on. I began to be more and more alarmed about crime among young people by young people.

As a local pastor I knew that my ministry was not just to encourage, feed and lead my congregation, but to help them engage with and contribute to the well-being of the community, the borough and the city. It was out of that passion and a sense of the challenge that faced the Church, together with two years of scoping work – engaging with mayors, chief constables, chief superintendents, social workers, probation officers, youth workers, Church and community leaders – that Street Pastors was born.

For me and a handful of others it also meant walking the streets in the early hours of the morning to meet 'nocturnal' people. I had to be where they were. I was stirred to learn that those people felt that the Church had a role to play in society; that it needed to look beyond its four walls and recognise that it had a ministry to the whole community. It was with all this information that we started Street Pastors.

We gave the initiative the name 'Street Pastors' because the Lord had helped us to see that our communities needed a shepherd carer. Back in April 2003 when the initiative was born and we started to walk the streets of Lambeth, I was pleasantly taken back by the warm reception I received. Someone said, 'How come it has taken the Church so long?' I am convinced that the words of Jesus written in the old hymn, 'Hold the fort, I am coming' are not actually an accurate picture of a Christian's place in the world. I believe God wants us to leave the comfort of our 'forts' and spend more time pastoring people on the streets.

In my 30 years of ministry, first as an itinerant evangelist, later as the pastor of a congregation, I know that many Christians up and down the land want to be empowered and encouraged to find their ministry – a ministry that will bring hope and peace and salvation to those within their community. For many of the members of our congregations do not want a pastoral role inside the Church, but feel they can express their faith in a more practical and relevant way outside the congregation. It has been a joy to meet people who are ready to work in their local community on a week-to-week, month-to-month and year-to-year basis.

In order to become a Street Pastor a person must be a member of a local church congregation and have a reference from their minister. They also need to be CRB checked and to have been trained through our training programme (50 hours of training over a six or seven month period). Street Pastors also need to be people who are willing to learn and serve. After training they are required to give one evening per month to walk on the streets in groups of four. They are there to engage with local people. Actually, often it's the other way around: people come up to Street Pastors, whichever city they might be in, and ask the same questions.

Who are you? What are you doing? Why are you doing it? Do you get paid? Street Pastors all over the country have been warmly received by people in their communities. In some areas nightclubs have collected money towards the training of Street Pastors, in one case, almost £4,000 in one evening!

Many Christians are interested to find out whether Street Pastors preach when they go out on the streets. Many Christians believe that unless you verbally communicate with people you are not truly representing the gospel to them. Yes, there is a time for us to proclaim the gospel of our Lord Jesus, but the reality is that people want to meet Christians who are showing them a *relevant* gospel. The Bible says, 'For God so loved the world that he gave ...' What did he give? He gave his son. That is the news of the gospel. Jesus came, Jesus gave and man's sins are forgiven. Street Pastors have many conversations on the streets often instigated by questions they are asked about what they believe and why. Out of those questions a Street Pastor can share his or her testimony of how Jesus has challenged them to be like him. When I go out as a Street Pastor, about 75% of the people I meet ask me to pray for them. Many say, 'I'm not religious, but say a prayer for me.' Street Pastors' teams are not only seeing a reduction in crime but are bringing hope and peace to needy people. Some people are receiving salvation.

As a Street Pastor I have spoken to many people about a huge variety of things in their life experience. When they ask why I am there, I say 'Because I care; because I want to listen to the needs and the voice of my community.' Street Pastors want to help their communities. Whatever the needs, we want to be able to help. Street Pastors is a holistic approach for our communities in the 21st century. Former Home Secretary, Jacqui Smith, was quoted in a newspaper as saying that she would like to see Street Pastors on every street in Britain. We have churches in every part of the UK, so I believe it is possible. We *can* be salt and light for our nation.

We need more Street Pastors, more Prayer Pastors and more School Pastors. Why don't you join us? By the way, our oldest Street Pastor is 88 years of age! You're never too old!

Rev Les Isaac
Director of Ascension Trust and Street Pastors.

For further information visit www.streetpastors.co.uk or email: info@streetpastors.org.uk

HOPEquotes: Solace

'Local churches provide the resources as we soothe hungry hearts with tea, cake and a smile at Isle of Wight music festivals. Our 'Solace' tent is space to chill, pray, or get feet washed. As people of hope we just give, as an expression of what God has given us, and convey his love and grace' [224]

224] Ced Wells, Solace Tent, Isle of Wight

DIVERT YOUR COURSE...

All too often we fail to listen because we have assumed that our own culture is normative, and that others should adapt to us. The gospel, by contrast, challenges us to do the adapting. Consider this conversation, a transcript of a 1995 radio exchange off the coast of Newfoundland between a US Navy vessel and some Canadians. Read the transcript and ask yourself how often, in different circumstances, you have been part of a similar conversation:

Canadians: Please divert your course 15 degrees to the south to avoid collision.

US Ship: Recommend you divert your course 15 degrees to the north to avoid collision.

Canadians: Negative. You will have to divert your course 15 degrees to the south to avoid a collision.

US Ship: This is the Captain of a US Navy ship. I say again, divert your course.

Canadians: Negative. I say again, you will have to divert your course.

US Ship: This is the aircraft carrier USS Lincoln, the second largest vessel in the United States Atlantic Fleet. We are accompanied by three destroyers, three cruisers and numerous support vessels. I demand that you change your course 15 degrees north. I say again 15 degrees north, or countermeasures will be undertaken to ensure the safety of this ship and its escort vehicles.

Canadians: We're a lighthouse. Your call. [225]

TAKE SPRING HARVEST HOME... TAKEAWAYS FROM HOPE

One of the things that has been a massive challenge for the HOPE initiative has been how to embrace the diversity of the body of Christ. What is the tangible expression to show that the gospel does break down prejudices and dividing walls, and that we can unite in Christ? To do this we have to learn to listen and be honest in our conversations about our differences. We need to recognise our unity in the gospel, with the great kaleidoscope of diversity of every tribe, tongue, people, nation, which will be brought before the throne in Revelation.

For instance, how many Christians who are not part of a Black Majority Church are aware that the Festival of Life gathers around 40,000 people at the Excel Centre for what is probably the largest prayer gathering in the UK, all praying for the revival of our nation? Are we aware that in many of our communities, where there is a breadth of diversity, there are people in each of those cultures who love Jesus and seek to serve him?

This session's Takeaway comes in the form of three simple but challenging questions:

1. How can I listen to others within my community who are from a different cultural setting? How can I discover how they do Church and live out their faith?

2. What can we do to celebrate our diversity and publicly declare our unity around the cause of Christ?

3. Is there a way that we can affirm, speak well of, and recognise the whole family of God within our community. Stories of HOPE, of where this has happened, are one of the best ways that non-believers see the gospel breaking down barriers.

Laurence Singlehurst and Roy Crowne, HOPE
www.hopetogether.org.uk

225] Released by the Chief of Naval Operations, Now at www.politicsforum.org, cited in Daniel Sinclair, *A Vision of the Possible: Pioneer Church Planting in Teams,* Authentic, 2005

CELEBRATE GOD'S BRILLIANT IDEA

This session of the *Theme Guide* has asked us to explore the breadth of God's family; all the different language and colours that will be drawn together into the Bride of Christ. We have envisaged worship in which the whole human family is involved; the many languages honouring one Lamb. We have asserted God's determination, from all the diverse human tribes, to make one new family. What can we celebrate in this brilliant idea?

1 We can rejoice that the Church is already the most ethnically and culturally diverse people-movement in history: that worship already rises to heaven in thousands of different languages.

2 We can celebrate the diversity of God's people here in the United Kingdom, as well as around the world: all the gifts that come into the Church from the many cultures God has drawn together.

3 We can thank God for his all-age, every-culture, room-for-everyone family. That there is a place for each of us. That we can enjoy being with people who are not like us. That we can express in our worship the exuberance of our diversity.

4 We can rejoice that there are no limits to the scope of God's project. Every tribe and tongue and language will be drawn in. The very ends of the earth will be included.

5 We can celebrate God's promise that a day is coming when

The earth will be filled with the knowledge of the glory of the LORD as the waters cover the sea... [226]

226] Habakkuk 2:14 NIV

ARTWORK CREDITS

David Dawes
www.daviddawes.co.uk
A graphic artist and web developer based in Sussex,
working with churches and charities.

Chris Gilbert
www.artandsoulman.co.uk
A freelance artist and speaker, Chris works in schools
and churches, using his artwork, music and humour to
communicate to all ages.

Theme Guide design by Mark Steel
www.lookatmark.com